ALIVE AND LOOSE
IN THE
ORDINARY

ALIVE AND LOOSE IN THE ORDINARY

Stories of the Incarnation

MARTHA STERNE

MOREHOUSE PUBLISHING

Morehouse Publishing, P.O. Box 1321, Harrisburg, PA 17105
Morehouse Publishing is an imprint of Church Publishing, Inc.

Cover art: © Royalty-Free/Corbis
Cover design: Corey Kent

Library of Congress Cataloging-in-Publication Data

Sterne, Martha.
  Alive and loose in the ordinary : stories of the incarnation / Martha Sterne.
    p. cm.
  ISBN -13: 978-0-8192-2155-1 (pbk.)
  1. Christian life—Anecdotes. 2. Incarnation—Anecdotes. I. Title.
  BV4501.3.S747 2006
  277.3'082—dc22

                              2005021660

Printed in the United States of America

06 07 08 09 10 11   6 5 4 3 2 1

For Mama and Muff

Contents

Preface

I AM IN THE KROGER, and I am looking at vinegars, very absorbed in the vinegars. And a woman is standing next to me and she is yelling into her cell phone and saying, "Darlin', I don't see the bacon ranch dressing. I see the buttermilk ranch, the chive ranch, the low-fat ranch, the regular ranch. I just don't see the bacon ranch—no, not anywhere, darlin'—don't see it at all."

I look over and spot the bacon ranch. And I gently tap the lady and point and mouth "bacon ranch." She grabs it. She never acknowledges me, looks at me, says thanks or spit or anything to me, but I hear her bellowing into the phone, "Darlin', praise the Lord, I have found the bacon ranch. Praise the Lord!"

I already have my face set to smile "You're welcome"—so not to be noticed as the discoverer of the bacon ranch prize is irritating. Not to mention the fact that I have lost my way on my own personal quest in the vinegars.

Sometimes we bray religious words past each other, and nobody finds what they are looking for. This can end up looking like Praising the Lord and Ignoring Your Neighbor. Our piety is often self-absorbed instead of communal, and abstract instead of fleshed and blooded. And so too often we do not connect with each other, much less live as one, which was always and ever Jesus' prayer.

Even in the grocery store, I think, when people help you find what you are looking for, you need to say thanks. And then praise the Lord for giving you the people who help you. Do you know the helpful ones I am talking about? They often look least likely to be of a bit of use. But Jesus says, *Ask, and it will be given you; seek, and you will find; knock, and the door will be opened.* And then he gives us to us for the seeking and asking and door opening. The process is very inefficient but what are you going to do? It has been my observation that God puts a disturbingly low priority on efficiency.

Of course we are not very efficient seekers either. Very few of us can name what we seek beyond the bacon ranch level. Occasionally I know what I am looking for but more often I am not able to name it. Faith? Peace? Personhood? Courage? Belonging? Calm? Jesus? Home?

So what amazes me day in and day out is the what-I-need gifts that show up in the parade of the day. It seems to me that what I am seeking can often be found by looking back over my shoulder at what was a nothing moment, even an irritating moment or a boring lull or a baffling misunderstanding. Or an oddly tender encounter. What looked like a waste of time has often been for me a blessing in hiding.

Except for once, I have never heard the voice of Jesus without some person or place in the creation doing the talking for him. So I want to witness to the power of the Incarnation alive and loose in the ordinariness of the world for us and through us and among us. And I offer these little sketches of remembered grace to invite you to notice your own soul's companions and the thin places in your life through which grace, well, springs.

This book is offered to the people—the fragile, the ornery, the almost dead, and the ghosts, and of course the grocery store shoppers—who over and over help me find the tender mercies I don't even know I am looking for. Thank you. And let me warn you: You are not through with your job. Praise the Lord.

The Traveler

Then the angel showed me the river of the water of life,
bright as crystal, flowing from the throne of God . . .

HE WAS SOMETHING ELSE. He was a small, fastidious man with a surprisingly strong and husky voice—a cross between a bark and a drawl. He was very deaf and he usually talked loud enough to hear himself.

By the time I knew him he was stroked up and down the left side of his body so that his mouth turned down to the left and his arm dangled close with the hand clawed inward. He shuffled slowly, listing forward with a pronounced limp, determined, resolute, on his way.

His wife was his steady companion and cared for him daily. She was also known in their circle of friends as Saint Virginia, for he had his ways and very firm opinions. He did not like change, and was undone if so much as a picture or a chair was moved to a different place in their home.

Duncan lived with great weakness from the stroke and then debilitating kidney disease for a long time. Since half of his body did not work very well he had a choice—to give in to invalidism and a very limited life, or to scrap his way into new methods and accommodations. He chose the latter.

He made a science of finding good parking places, and he and Virginia went where they wanted to, including to church, where

<3>3</3>

Duncan sat in the same pew every week. If anyone by some horrible mistake chose to sit in his place, well, he handled it. Though he is dead now, we probably should put a sign on the pew for the next few years—reserved—just in case.

He kept up with a lot of friends. There wasn't a day that went by—even to almost the end—that he did not stay curious and interested in others. He asked me every time I saw him how someone was who had just come into his mind. I have witnessed only a few times this interest in the lives of others even toward the end of one's own life. Curiosity is a gift of the Holy Spirit, and Duncan stayed curious.

He was an artist in needlepoint. His eye for detail, his commitment to one stitch and then the next, his fierce desire for it to be right—whatever "it" was—was just remarkable. His utter concentration sustained him when the stroke left him, for most purposes, diminished. Really, his one-sidedness should have taken him completely out of the needle-pointing business, but he invented a contraption to hold the cloth in a frame at just the right angle and distance. And then he poked that needle into each tiny square opening, one after another after another. (I don't know how he tied off the knots.) And the hours would go by.

He needle-pointed his way around his house, and eventually he needle-pointed his way across the church, so that now every time we share Eucharist, his splendid needlework pillow supports the altar book that the priest uses for prayer. And every time we kneel for communion we kneel on Tennessee wildflowers threaded into all the liturgical seasons by him and some others.

Three years before his death, he said he needed a new project to go out on, a big one. And so we said we needed a parish banner, a big one. He sniffed and thought about it and said that would do. Then an artist in the parish drew and worked out on graph paper an amazing swirl of five loaves and two fishes, the feastly sign of abundance even when the pickings are looking slim. He critiqued and recritiqued every line and every color skein selection. The long-suffering artist, who had not realized that she would become a full-time body slave, grinned and bore it gracefully and trekked back and forth to the yarn store for months.

Now every time we look at our parish banner—his beautiful even stitches, over a million needle piercings filling out the artist's holy design—well, we keep telling the story of its one-handed, single-minded creation. It took him a year, and I wondered if he would live to finish it. That was wasted worry, for he not only needed to finish it; he also gave himself a couple of years to receive the accolades.

He told us that he wanted his ashes scattered in one of our mountain streams because he always loved to travel and that way he will be traveling forever. A few days after he died, four of us went out on a cloudy morning to the Little River that cascades down from the Great Smokies and meanders through our county. I didn't know if he would get his wish to travel or just sink to the bottom of the streambed, but we said a prayer asking God to watch over him and bring him home. His son stood on a rock and leaned down into the water and opened the sack. And for maybe a minute, the ashes hung suspended in a little pool and then slowly spread and streamed forward, with grace, streaming and seeking to return to the source. So help me, the sun came out.

We watched for a long time, and even when we left there was a faint glinting trail of Duncan traveling on and finding his way home forever.

For Your Reflection

Remember ornery people you love and why.
What keeps your spirit alive?

Beauty Parlors

For now we see in a mirror, dimly, but then we will see face to face.

1 CORINTHIANS 13:12

I HAVE ALWAYS HAD DIFFICULT HAIR. I want to be grateful for the hair God has given me so I'll just use the word difficult, meaning frizzly or flat, depending on the weather and my current life stance—more like a mood ring than a reliable head of hair. I was radically towheaded as a child and green-headed if I spent a lot of time in chlorinated swimming pools. Then it turned blue when I was a teenager due to a bottle of some nasty stuff that I thought surely would make me look glamorous. I haven't tried dyeing it since, though a member of my parish's search committee said the first thing a couple of folks asked her when I came to East Tennessee was, Do you think she dyes her hair? I said, Well, I hope I'd do a better job than this.

Due to having difficult hair, I notice the fortitude and kindness of people who cut hair—people who look into the mirrors with us through thick and thin. I remember the barber, Cecil by name, who gave our three-year-old son his first real hair cut. Huge crocodile tears—the boy, and not far behind mama and daddy—and Cecil just kept murmuring: My boy, I believe you're a baseball player. Hit that ball a mile. You can hit that ball a mile, Charlie. And the little boy heard the words—you're a baseball player—and looked in the mirror and stopped seeing the scissors and hearing the whuuzzzz of the clippers and saw instead baseball player

7

Charlie—we'd always called him Charles, but now he'd heard the word and now he saw Charlie the baseball player who could hit that ball a mile.

Or some years later, I was going to Grady, who every time I walked in the door of the beauty parlor always screamed in mock horror, Emergency, Emergency! Only this time I am not kidding around. I have been doing—sometimes very poorly—a jobs ministry in an Atlanta public housing project, and I have seen more than comfortable, middle-class people ever want to see about the grind and the pain in the prison of generations of poverty. And I don't talk about that, but I say Grady, I either need a totally new haircut or a totally new me and right now I don't care which. And without saying a word, he cut off every hair of my head—almost like the ceremony when someone enters monastic orders. And he swung the chair around. And he said, You don't need a new you. You need to be you, and God knows that'll be enough. And you know what? He was right.

Or my mother's friend, Tara, in Jackson, Mississippi, who cut hair all week and then she and her husband—both white people— played the piano and sang in a black gospel choir on Sunday. They didn't sit around and deplore the fact that Sunday morning is the most segregated hour in American life. They went to a black church and got in ministry with African-Americans and had a ball. Then off and on through the week she talked about her church with her customers, looking into the mirror with them as they heard her words and saw new possibilities for doing church and loving the Lord.

And when my father got kind of down after retirement, she heard that his secret dream was to be a country music songwriter. And Tara and her husband recorded his one and only "Meet Me at the Mail Box Molly," a tragic tune of love and flood. Oh, did he get a kick out of that. Now after Tara has retired she comes to my

mother's house and she sits Mama in front of the mirror in her
bathroom and together Lord knows what they see and say but I bet
you they know they are beautiful.

Or lately, which is what got me thinking about all this haircut
business, I went to Mary to get my hair cut and as I am paying and
walking out the door, I hear her say to her next customer, just before
the young helper starts the shampooing, How's your husband? And
the woman, probably in her mid sixties says, Oh Mary, we're in a
bad way. He calls me ten, fifteen times a day at work. He says there
is something wrong, that I have to come home. But he doesn't
know what's wrong. And he wants to go to the emergency room
and they can't ever find anything. And he cries my name in the
night, and I don't know what to do. And with that, everything
stops. Mary signals the shampoo girl to wait, and she kneels before
the distraught woman, who's weeping now, and says, Tell me. And
I left, love and comfort and common sense flowing through the
room like the balm of Gilead.

You know the church could do worse than be an "inner beauty"
shop—a place where we can look into the mirror together and see
each other's potential and belovedness. The church could do worse
than be a place where love is shared and truth is told and the beauty
of becoming is the work of the community.

For Your Reflection

Who looks in the mirror with you?
Where are your inner beauty shops?

Growing Up, Starting
on White Street

But speaking the truth in love, we must grow up in every way
into him who is the head, into Christ.

EPHESIANS 4:15

MY FATHER'S PARENTS DIED, one after the other, when he was a teenager. First the overworked country doctor father, who smoked like a chimney, died of a heart attack, and then the invalid mother died six months later of chronic kidney disease and, I guess, a broken heart.

They lived on White Street in Alexandria, Louisiana, and I am named for my father's mother—Martha Adams Packer. I see her picture and I think I believe I look like you—something in the set of the mouth, and the eyes. She was funny and taught children to play the piano. My grandfather, Dr. Joseph Alexander Packer, delivered babies and sewed people up and watched over them, waiting to see what would happen. What more could a doctor do in those days?

I catch flashes of the two of them—just flashes—the men in our family being docs, for instance. And when I look in the mirror I see just that glimmer of her face. And, of course, when I remember my father, I know how he loved them and I wonder how the loss of them so early shaped his soul. Here is what I know of them, of where I come from—through the prism of what I know of my father.

My father was called Sonny until my mother got hold of him and he became Jim. When he was orphaned at fifteen, sixteen.

11

Daddy's older sister and her husband moved from their dairy farm to the house on White Street to make a home for him until he got out of high school. And then his sisters sent him to the University of the South up on The Mountain, as they say, in Tennessee, where he was embraced by several professors and their families and other students. He always said Sewanee was one of the happiest times of his life and hinted that the absence of women had been a plus. I wish he had lived to see his granddaughter graduate from there.

After leaving Sewanee a year early to save money, he headed on to medical school at Tulane. My mother, in the meantime, had had her eye on him since she was twelve. She persevered over a long haul and many obstacles. I know this because I saw their high school annual and the caption under his picture read—*Wanted but Not Got*. Mother worked that out.

The war loomed; they married; and he left not too long after for training maneuvers out West. Mother sweet-talked her sister into going with her in an unair-conditioned car in August to California so that he could see his six-week-old daughter, my older sister, before he left for Europe. The baby, who had good sense, wailed in the throbbing heat the whole way. But he saw her.

By the time he was twenty-six, twenty-seven, he was captain over a medical company attached to an armored division in the thick of it in France and Belgium and Germany, eventually the Battle of the Bulge. So ten years from orphaned boy to field doc and leader of men in that horrific, bloody war. He talked about freezing winters, how cold he was, never about the blind butchery of war that he had to deal with every day.

I can't imagine having to grow up that fast. I consider my own pleasant path and I marvel at the stamina of those who early on live through family catastrophe or chronic chaos. I marvel at those who lived through the Depression and World War II and Korea, as well as those whose lives intersected with Vietnam, a war fought on two fronts—there and here. Now we see that pain again. But sometimes that's how it goes—people get jerked into adulthood, surviving profound loss and being put to the test early, early on. I wish it would never happen that way, but it does. For individuals and for communities, sometimes you have to grow up real fast. The early Christian community, for instance.

So even though we pray "Save us from the time of trial," sometimes the trial comes early. For others—me, for instance—growing up seems to be more of an option, not crisis driven and maybe, on the surface, not very necessary. Yet really, growing up is why we are born—to become all that we are created to be, the only you, the only me that God ever makes, each of us growing up into the fullness of Christ.

What does growing up look like? I think about the grown-ups who raised me—my father and my mother—and I think growing up looks like this: making your own choices and taking responsibility for them, no longer tossed to and fro by the winds of others' opinions.

I think growing up looks like endurance.

I think growing up looks like comfort with shades of gray; grown-ups, no matter if they are nineteen or ninety, can tolerate ambiguity.

And growing up means the willingness to offer your gifts and the ability to survive when your gifts are rejected.

And growing up is coping with the unexpected, even with miracles, which are wonder-full but hard on the nerves.

And growing up in Christ looks like, above all and in all, the capacity for giving and receiving love, especially agape love—self-offering love, which is to stretch out beyond yourself toward God, toward your neighbor, to be a human being at full stretch like the One who *stretched out his arms upon the cross and offered himself for the whole world.*

I think my father woke up just amazed to be alive just about every day of his grown-up life. After so much loss and death and destruction early on, it's no wonder. And some have told me that when one lives years and years more than one's parents lived, as my father lived on and on past his early fifties, well, that's great but bewildering.

At any rate he was glad to be alive and loved his family and friends and the drama of ordinary days and the delights of good food and the endearing and ridiculous peculiarities of the human condition. When he retired in his seventies, he started working as a volunteer on the Contact Crisis line in Jackson. I told him, Daddy, don't call the women "honey" anymore; that's not the way you do it nowadays. But I'm sure he did call them honey and I'm even more sure it didn't matter. Because he was reaching out, stretching out the best he could as a child of God growing up even in his old age, trying to mature the best he could into the full stature of Christ.

I hope I carry just a little part of his gentle, ironic presence with me everywhere I go, every day of my life. And always standing behind him, the parents on White Street. And behind them, who knows? We are made of clay from so many strata.

For Your Reflection

What does growing up look like to you?
What do you know about the clay from which you are formed?
Whom do you hope you resemble?

Courtship and Marriage

Arise, my love, my fair one, and come away.

O my dove, in the clefts of the rock, in the covert of the cliff,

let me see your face, let me hear your voice;

for your voice is sweet, and your face is lovely.

SONG OF SOLOMON 2:13b–14

COURTSHIP IS STRANGE. But you knew that.

It is early April and my husband and a tom turkey have a thing. They have been gobbling at each other for a couple of weeks— Carroll standing in the screen porch in the spring dusk-dark with a stick and rubber band turkey caller. He sounds not cute—sort of like givvgivvlgivvvegivvvvllll—to me but what do I know about the affairs of the heart of a turkey? The tom hides on the rhododendron bank by the creek and answers again and again—urgent, yearning, a deeper tone—gawwrrrbbblgarwwwwrrrrbbblllblllllll-gawwwrrr.

The turkey goes to sleep finally, thank God. And we have supper—chicken.

This morning he is back, now in the open on the gravel drive— the turkey, that is. Carroll has gone to work. His swain gobbles and peers at the house—the tail spreading a huge Indian lady's fan— mink brown at the base shading lighter and lighter and then a gold rim around the top edges of the feathers. He fluffles every feather on his body—a ruff appears around his neck, just like

Shakespeare—only the ruff is dark, almost black. Down his chest
hangs a strange, feathered beard that looks like a fifties-era skinny
necktie.

When the sun hits his back at the right angle, he glistens as if
anointed with oil. Such radiance demands attention. I am scared
to try the turkey call because the last time I did he flew off appalled.
So I sit silent at the window, while his wing feathers trail to the
ground and he takes little mincing steps toward the Honda. One
step, two step, three, pause. Gawwwbbblgarwwbbblllbblllll. I think
he thinks Carroll is in the car.

His neck turns bright pink-red, an impossible shade, the color
and shape of a long, sun-bleached red balloon. His head is now
turquoise blue and crowned with white—all rising above the red
throat like an abstract of an American flag. He stretches now
toward the house and lets loose the longest most loving gobble yet.
He quicksteps again, closer, closer. Perhaps he has decided the girl
of his dreams is in here—and oh I wish she were—waiting for him
with open wings. Such ardor deserves response.

He does the three-step thing again and again. One step, two step,
three, pause. Head cocked. He minces back and forth, back and
forth—half an hour goes by—and I am transfixed. I love him but I
don't think that helps his situation. He lifts his head, listening,
watching, yearning in every fiber of his fat fluffled being. Then one
step, two step, pause.

Occasionally he wilts. Feathers down, tail feathers literally dragging. The colors fade. Is he discouraged? But only for the moment.

There are three female turkeys that hang out around our place,
one quite lame who has survived the winter, to our surprise. One
of the girls moseys by on her way to the backyard where we as usual
have scattered cracked corn. He follows at a distance and watches
her eat—he doesn't eat a bite, not a nibble—fanning himself and
occasionally gobbling, though really more gurgling. She pays him

no mind. None. She pecks at the corn, scratches her feet in the leaves, and as a rule faces away from him.

He stands there still. In all his fine array. She is picking nits out of her feathers as if to say, Sorry, I have to wash my hair.

This is ridiculous. I have got to go. I have an appointment with a couple who want to get married. She has been and so has he. They think they know what went wrong the other times, which is good. I hope they know what they are getting into. But who ever knows?

I can promise you no priest or minister or counselor knows who is going to make it, who is not. I meet with people for "premarital instruction" and we usually have a wonderful time while we talk through issues around money and in-laws and such. I often wonder, though—particularly with the young ones fixated on the wedding and the wounded ones desperate to put loneliness behind them— I wonder if we ever do truly address the realities and demands of lifelong commitment.

Courtship is so easy. Marriage is so daily.

I always ask them to memorize their vows so that four or five years down the road when they are ready to kill each other they will perhaps remember what it was they said they would do. Which is: *to have and to hold from this day forward, for better for worse, for richer for poorer, in sickness and in health, to love and to cherish, until we are parted by death.*

So today I will meet this couple. And we will keep talking about the marriage. And of course the wedding. And they will walk out the door, as have so many other couples, and I know that half of them statistically speaking are on their way to getting a divorce.

We are great at courtship. Who in the world has ever seen a culture so committed to courtship? But we are lousy, lousy, lousy at marriage. And I think we are lousy at marriage because men and women do not have a clue as to how to keep vows. And the church does not seem to know how to help. After the courtship, after the

wedding, in sometimes no time at all, men and women are break-
ing their vows, most often by committing adultery. Adultery is what
breaks up most marriages in my world, and adultery is a sin which
Jesus named and worried about. He never, by the way, said a
mumbling word about sexual orientation, just about faithfulness.

Heterosexuals have made such an ungodly mess of marriage, I
would think we would rejoice to hear that there are people who
want to try to rehabilitate the institution. From where I sit, gay
marriage is not some blessing of promiscuity and free-love life
style; it is the opposite, a very conservative strategy and a discipline
of faithfulness.

As a gay man told me, "Doesn't everybody know we are great at
fixing up old houses?" Who can tell? They might fix up this old
house as well.

I am strangely hopeful that the hysterics and hullabaloo around
gay marriage may herald the dawn of a new day for all marriage.
We may be beginning—very awkwardly and fearfully—to reach
way back into the heart of what it means to make a faithful,
monogamous, lifelong commitment to another person and go on
together from there.

The turkeys have wandered off and I turn my mind to the couple I am meeting. I hope they pay attention to each other beyond
the first flush of hormones. I hope he won't be narcissistic. I hope
she won't be nitpicky. If they are going to make a nest together, I
hope they will be faithful to each other and honor the One who
made them and invites them to be one.

For Your Reflection

Courtship is one thing; marriage is another. How do we do
both better?

How do we help each other be faithful?

A Way in the Manger

*And she gave birth to her firstborn son and wrapped him in
bands of cloth, and laid him in a manger. . . .*

LUKE 2:7

A PARISHIONER TOLD ME that he went to our chapel altar for
prayers of healing on a summer Sunday a while back. And the healer
said an odd, unseasonal prayer—"May you take the manger with
you." The person said he had been hoping for the guidance of the Holy
Spirit and that he thought the Holy Spirit was more of a mature, take-
charge, get-it-all-together official Spirit of Holiness who told you
just what to do. And instead he was told to take the manger with him.

What on earth did the healer mean? Perhaps to keep connected
to the humility of Christ? Perhaps to look for newness of life?
Perhaps to acknowledge the profound and somewhat terrifying
vulnerability that God has shown to us and for us?

Or maybe to know that we get born anew in some very odd
places. I don't know what the healer meant when she said to take
the manger with you but the image has stuck with me.

The words took me back thirty years to our first neighborhood
as a married couple. Our first house was a weird, ancient, and tiny
stucco thing—2006 Gerda Terrace—in a neighborhood cut out of
an old orange grove in the middle of Orlando, Florida. There was
a lake at the bottom of the street and the grocery store was in walking distance and the bus ran right past our house, which was
good because we only had one car. My husband was the national

accounts department of the bank. Literally, he was it. I am sure they chose him because of his potential and his winning personality but also because he was twenty-five and young and dumb enough to think it was thrilling to slog around to three cities in two days.

So he would pack up his suitcase—with his first and last triple-polyester wrinkle-free suit—and get on the bus and head to the airport to call on customers in Philadelphia and Houston and Kansas City. And I would stay behind with our firstborn—the one who did not sleep through the night until he was two—and Jake, the dog who was supposed to be a watchdog but whose only home defense strategy would have been licking burglars to death.

For me, the early motherhood era was an incompetent, lonely time. Carroll knew what he was doing with the baby since he had little sisters and had babysat a lot more than me. Our neighbors also seemed to be people who understood the world and had their places firmly entrenched in it. Mr. Todd was retired and refinished furniture in his garage, and his wife bustled around and everything there looked as neat as a pin. Mrs. Steffens was the dignified librarian who walked her little white poodle at the same times every day, and he never did bad things in people's yards. One man was the principal of the high school so of course he knew everything.

Even the people in the pink house across the street—a grandmother, a mom, and a horribly spoiled little boy—seemed to have it all together. I remember them vividly because they had a boa constrictor named Bud that went missing. Everybody else in the neighborhood seemed to take his disappearance in stride. I on the other hand was paralyzed by the possibilities of his dropping off the big oak tree in our front yard on me or the baby carriage, or hiding in my laundry room. Bud, by the way, showed up three months later on their front steps. And the grandmother swore he knocked.

So an ordinary neighborhood. You have lived there, may live there now. It was one of those places where you don't know each other well, but people's public habits are acceptable, and there is order. To my lonely eyes, everybody on Gerda Terrace seemed to know just where they belonged, even the snake, and just how to live their life. Everyone except me. I loved my husband, loved the little baby although that love was tested sorely in the dark hours of the night. And I liked walking by the lake and exchanging little pleasantries. "Hot enough for ya?" "Oooh the baby's grown!" Like that.

But I thought is this what life is? Pleasantries exchanged with semi-strangers? Cleaning this and cooking that? Reading books about toilet training? Constantly waiting for Carroll to get back from Poughkeepsie or wherever so my real life could recommence? Maybe you've never done that, but a lot of the rest of us have—lots of us have lived our lives waiting to live our lives.

And so it has been my personal experience and my observation as a pastor that, in the immortal words of Auntie Mame, life is a banquet and most poor suckers are starving to death. And isn't it lonely to starve to death in the middle of the banquet?

I think of another young woman—no house, no husband, no car, no grocery store, no lake, no neighbors, no order, no pleasantries exchanged. No life really as middle-class folks understand life. She had nothing—except the Holy Spirit quickening, quickening in the secret depths of her mind and her soul and her body. And that is all it took.

And if we are blessed, we remember that what happened to her can happen to us. Holy, full, new life, like the carol says, can be born in us any day. For Mary found the manger where new life could be nourished and so can we. Not all-in-order life, not everything completed and fixed and done, the end. But new life—for when you go to the manger you go to the source of life—which is love, and there you will be fed.

That is what happened to me in Orlando. I found the manger. Not in a church but in a neighbor's home. Her name was Marcia— Mar-see-ah—very tiny and very pregnant. She was a Nicaraguan refugee, her family having been driven out in one of the revolutions. Carroll said don't ask too many questions because he thought they were on the bad guy side. That sure didn't matter to me.

Her Midwestern engineer husband was gone even more than Carroll, and her English was very awkward and her little wire-rim glasses were often askew, and she was kindness and tea. Her dog was huge and much worse than mine—he was a Russian wolfhound and she talked to him in Spanish—and she knew what to do with all the oranges, and she wasn't that great of a housekeeper, and she loved to read. And when their little baby, Donald-cito, was born, I got to make a gooey casserole for them and tell her what meager baby things I knew.

And she and I—we kept close to the manger and did not just exchange pleasantries. And we loved the beginnings in our lives and we stayed close to the source. Which turns out to be not a creed to recite or a litmus test to pass; instead the source is always love and is always bubbling up somewhere in your life and mine if we will but look for the manger and keep it close.

It turns out that the manger is anywhere that peace lays down his sweet head. Anywhere gentle life is being nourished. Anywhere love is being spoken in the language of your heart. That is the way and the truth and the life, a way in the manger.

Be near me, Lord Jesus; I ask thee to stay
close by me for ever, and love me I pray.
Bless all the dear children in thy tender care,
and fit us for heaven to live with thee there.

For Your Reflection

Where have the mangers been in your life?
Where is your life nurtured now?

Behold Your Mother

Then he said to the disciple, "Here is your mother."

JOHN 19:27

PALM SUNDAY SOME YEAR back in Atlanta, I don't remember which. But we are doing our thing—having our annual dramatic reading of the passion story, and it is going particularly well this year. We practiced hard and it shows. The narrator is great. Jesus knows his lines. Peter is a cowardly lion. Pilate is ironic and effete and I am just enjoying the show.

And then the part comes when Pilate says what he says every year. What do you want me to do with this man? This is the signal for the whole congregation to get in on the action. And the crowd yells, CRUCIFY HIM! CRUCIFY HIM! Bloodcurdling effect. Very satisfactory.

And while the crowd's pretended rage is still ringing in our ears, from about two-thirds back in the pews, comes a woman's voice bellowing. NO. NO. NO. Not my Boy. No. Don't. Not my Boy. And then sobs throbbing through the air to break your heart.

We are appalled, deeply appalled. What had been an audience is becoming something else. What is happening? For God's sake, what is going on? Somehow 400 observers are transformed into a body of witnesses.

I crane my neck and see that someone sitting near her comforts her. Well, thank God. They look for all the world like Mary and John lost at the foot of the cross, her head collapsed on the shoulder of her pew-mate, whose name, I remember, is actually John.

We sit in silence, all of us, for a timeless time. For what had been a well-done scripted and rehearsed play has become *anamnesis,* has become Real Presence. And the veil of the temple is torn in two. She is there at the foot of the cross. Perhaps you would have diagnosed her as mentally ill or maybe drunk—but she is there and she is our host and takes us there too.

Finally, the rector stands up with tears in his eyes and says, Sometimes it causes you to tremble. Tremble. Tremble. And we begin the prayers.

What if we had ushered her out? What a loss. But we didn't and she was peculiar and beautiful and rich with gifts to give and plugged into the power like I've never seen before. Where else would such a woman belong on Palm Sunday during the Passion of Our Lord but in the Body of Christ?

God bless her and God bless the disciple who held her and God bless us all, lost in the mystery on our better days.

For Your Reflection

Have you ever experienced a peculiar holy person? Who and how? What would it mean to be lost in the mystery?

Embracing Your Fears

God made the wild animals of the earth of every kind, and
the cattle of every kind, and everything that creeps upon the
ground of every kind. And God saw that it was good.

GENESIS 1:25

OKAY, I AM TAKING A WALK with a friend who is an artist, physical therapist, and child of God. The grass is greening and the sun is shining and all is right with the world and we are idly chatting about this and that.

She does a little gaspy intake of breath, and there about a step ahead of us on the path is a striped snake. I would say about a forty-foot-long snake. I prepare to wheel and run, but my friend says, Look. Look in its mouth. And I force myself to look and there sticking out of the monster's mouth are two froggy legs. Moving. Not thrashing. Picture frog legs doing calisthenics. And then, horrified, I look even closer and there are also two little froggy arms almost embracing the cheeks of the snake—sort of patting the snake and then sagging helpless and then patting again.

The frog's head of course was heading down the snake's gullet. I say to my friend, who I have come to believe can handle just about any situation, Do you think you can pull the little guy out of the snake? And she says quickly and firmly that she just doesn't believe she can do that. She does, however, pick up a few little pebbles and toss them gently around the snake, as if that will do any good.

We are mesmerized. The determined frog-leg calisthenics, the little frog arms embracing the executioner, and the snake himself, in a peristaltic ecstasy, swaying his whole body side to side like the plump tail of a satisfied pussycat.

This goes on and on and on and then out of nowhere, all of a sudden, the snake halts the side winding, unhinges his jaws, gives a little burp, and spits out the frog. The frog picks himself up, dusts himself off, and hops off into the grass none the worse for wear.

My friend's theory is that the frog puffed up his buccinator muscles like Louis Armstrong blowing the horn, and in the process cut off the snake's air supply. Whatever, it was an amazing self-rescue.

The snake sits for a while, his tongue flicking, and then sidles over to the other side of the path. If he had shoulders he would have shrugged them. For it is true: you win some, you lose some. We watch him slide into the grass, disappearing en route to his next luncheon appointment.

I am taking this to heart. And if I can stand still and watch a snake and learn from it, then you can, too. Just keep on putting one foot in front of the other. Embrace your fears. Blow your own horn. And don't ever, ever, ever give up. You were made for freedom.

(Of course if you are rooting for the snake, better luck next time.)

For Your Reflection

What would embracing your fears look like?

Is there a frog in your throat that you would be better off spitting out?

In the Valley of the Shadow

*Yeah though I walk through the valley of the shadow of
death, I will fear no evil: for thou art with me; thy rod
and thy staff they comfort me.*

PSALM 23:4 (KJV)

I HAVE WALKED INTO A LOT of hospital rooms and sat beside a lot
of hospital beds in my time. Except for having babies and broken
arms and getting rid of wisdom teeth, I never had the experience
of being sat by in a hospital room until I reached my fifty-sixth
year. Nowadays of course I would have had the arms and the teeth
handled in somebody's office, and the babies would have been
drive-through service.

Besides, I like it worlds better when I am the beside-bed sitter.

Here is what happened. I was ending the first leg of a three-
month sabbatical and had been staying with family in various ports
of call in Mississippi. My husband had flown in for the weekend
and we had houseguests at my family's old place in the country
outside of Natchez. It was a cool gray May morning and we drove
into town and parked on Main, across the street from my great-
grandmother's house, which had morphed into a grocery store and
now it's gone, too. Our destination was my favorite park where, in
the dappled light and shadows of moss-draped giant oaks, a huge
triple-decker fountain quietly splashes with the fattest, reddest goldfish in the world. I have loved that particular fountain and those
goldfish for fifty years, and I wanted to show them off.

We were strolling into the park and I just fell out. Well, first I turned beet red and walked into a wall and then I fell out. All I can remember is a sensation of white fog coming in as if a mosquito-spray truck had just driven into my head. Slam, bam, on the pavement out cold. Labored breathing, now turning fish-belly white, wetting pants, and over and around all of it just plain out cold. This was reported obviously at a later time by my husband and the friends (who tactfully left out that I had wet my pants).

I have no memory of the twenty minutes or so on the sidewalk. The men in the party began calm and confident that I would snap out of it. The woman, a friend since kindergarten, watched for two or three minutes and then said to a passerby, Call 911. Thank God. I mean I don't want to be sexist, but it is one thing not to ask for directions (which the males in my life never do). This was another thing.

The ambulance came and they fiddled with me and finally got me going by means of harassment—sticking a breathing tube down my throat, which never had to be activated because the mere outrage of the intrusion brought me around. I have no memory of the ambulance ride with the siren screaming, which just makes me furious, but I was talking and, according to my husband, making a serious attempt to direct the medical team. Politely but firmly.

When we got to the hospital, I evidently told my husband that I was always really, really glad we got married and then I asked him what time it was. I fixated on these two things, which are of course primal realities—time and relationship—and brought them back up again about every minute and a half. Finally my husband made my old kindergarten friend come into the little emergency bay and tell me what time it was for a while, until she said, I already told you that, now think about something else, which is what old friends are for. She says I did think about something else, though no telling what. I bet I was thinking I am glad I'm not dead.

I have no memory of the emergency room and very little memory of the two days in the unit in the hospital that followed. Actually I was not what you would call a deep thinker for the next four or five weeks due to this experience, since all our brains like oxygen all of the time—not just some of the time—all the time. My husband, however, knew that I was going to be fine from the moment one of my Natchez cousins came by to check on me in the hospital, and I whispered to him that I thought a couple of tamales from the good place would help the situation. I couldn't get the name of the place out but after all I live out of town and he knew where to go.

My brother, who is a doctor in Denver, kept up by telephone, and his advice was Martha, don't take any more damn sabbaticals.

As an aside, I disagree. Normally sabbaticals are refreshing, I believe we would live in a safer, holier, more delight-filled, world if we practiced at least weekly Sabbath, the most overlooked and abused commandment in the Big Ten roundup, and the most countercultural demand from God in our day. The Sabbath message is Stop. You and your production don't keep the world turning. You are not in charge. Stop.

I got it.

Evidently a big allergic reaction had cascaded through my systems. On one level it doesn't really matter what threw me into a hospital bed. It was one of those things that comes to take up residence in you in your middle age and probably won't go away. I will be having checkups and taking shots and trying to get off pills for the foreseeable future, just like a lot of you who may read this page are doing for different ailments right now. Unless you die young and suddenly, that is the way it goes for insured Americans. And we are the lucky ones. Without medical resources, people don't go through the hassle of chronic diseases. They just die.

Some theologians describe the Fall, when Adam and Eve disobeyed God and lost paradise, as the Fall Upward because ever since they bit the apple, human consciousness has been blessed and cursed by knowing about the limits. Such as: We don't live in paradise and we don't live forever. Nobody does. Now having taken my own little fall I know up close and personal that stumbling against those realities offers some blessings. Unless you die suddenly and young, you will fall against your limits, too. You may walk into different walls and ruefully discover different blessings, but walls have a lot in common and blessings are all cousins, aren't they?

I think I am in the middle of my story. Maybe that is where you think you are. But any of us could get hit by a truck tomorrow or we could live to be 114 and be a gift and a tribulation to our great-great-grandchildren. The truth is we are always walking toward home in the valley of the shadow. And we might just as well learn to be at home there, too. For yea, when you walk through the valley, every once in a while, in the rocky places where you stumble, you just may catch a glimpse of the shadow of the Shepherd. For he is with you and his rod and his staff will comfort you.

For Your Reflection

Have you walked through the valley of the shadow? What was the terrain?

Are there some blessings from the walk?

We Never Could Walk on Water

*So Peter got out of the boat, started walking on the water, and came
toward Jesus. But when he noticed the strong wind, he became
frightened, and beginning to sink, he cried out, "Lord, save me!"*

MATTHEW 14:29–30

I WAS ORDAINED TO THE PRIESTHOOD in Atlanta on the evening
of April 4, 1989, although almost not. The weather had been
strange all day—heavy, sullen air and brownish clouds and then
about four o'clock all hell broke loose and eleven little tornadoes
touched down around the city and just tore the place up. The TV
stations were hysterical, with news crews out all over the place and
I was at home pulling myself together and getting dressed—praying
that the church had electricity. Never mind the health and safety of
the citizens of Atlanta, I was getting ordained, by God, and one has
to maintain one's priorities even when, especially when eleven
tornadoes touch down.

The bishop calls and whines. He says, I have spent the last forty-
five minutes under my desk. And he whimpers—Do we have to go
through with this thing? He had been my parish priest and hadn't
looked like very good bishop material to me and he hadn't ordained
anyone yet so I wasn't even sure he knew how to do it. So though I
wanted to hiss, Get your chicken self out from under the desk right
now, I remembered he was the bishop and I needed him at this particular moment so I said, Please get out from under the desk. And
then I heard his secretary and his wife laughing in the background.

31

They showed up, as did a few brave others, and outside of his saying—when everybody laid hands on top of my head—outside of his saying, Therefore, Father, through Jesus Christ your Son give your Holy Spirit to "Margaret," it all went fine. Just like most ordinations—those that happen to the one on purpose and those that happen to the family by contagion, sort of like getting the flu. For when you live with an ordained person, you catch it, one way or the other. Normally ordinations all go fine. The tricky part is living into that which was already spoken, in the same way you are called to live into your baptism. Jesus actually was ordained at his baptism, as are we all. It is just that for some it takes an extra go-around.

In most Episcopal dioceses we renew our ordination vows every Lent, though my friend Gene, my predecessor in Maryville, said he doesn't think we need to come together every year to renew our vows. He says, Forget coming together to renew—instead we need to come together to repent. I forgot to ask him whether he meant to repent getting ordained or repent slopping it up.

I suspect, however, every time ordained people hear again how it is our task to proclaim by word and deed the Gospel and to fashion our lives according to the Gospel, and when we hear again how we are supposed to love and serve all the people—the young and the old, the strong and the weak, the rich and the poor—I suspect we all quiver. I mean I can love hard. But I sure can dislike hard too. And be petty about it.

And I suspect every time we hear how we are to nourish Christ's people from the riches of his grace—every time we hear all that again—I hope we have the grace to wince. For sometimes we forget to trust the riches of grace and instead try to puff up as big as we can to look like we are strong and trustworthy and capable and nurturing. I don't know about other clergy, but I can fool a lot of the people a lot of the time. Then sometimes I lie awake in the night and have the decency to be ashamed.

Do you remember when Dorothy and her friends got to Emerald City and went to the palace and the Wizard of Oz is great and terrifying and his voice shakes the rafters and they tremble in fear until the little dog Toto pulls back a small curtain to reveal just a little old bald man pretending to be a wizard? And he says, I'm not a bad man; I am just a bad wizard. And lots of clergy know what he means.

We are not very good wizards. And we are not very good martyrs. We are positively lousy at being saviors. As a wise old fox of a priest said to me in the midst of one of those strange skirmishes about paint color in the narthex or something equally profound— the old fox said, Jesus died for the sins of the church. That's been done. And now I'm not gonna.

And every time we try to be savvy politicians sooner or later it backfires, for me usually in the space of about ten minutes and two phone calls. And though the books tell us to be nonanxious presences and self-differentiated leaders, we are very often not. And we get triangulated all the time because we are too dumb to see it coming. Heck, I start the triangles half the time.

And we are not doctors so we can't give a pill or cut somebody up and take something bad out—tempting as that may seem. And we are not lawyers—thank God for small favors—though my lawyer friends say the same back. And we would make terrible judges—how impossible would that task be sitting where we sit, looking at that sea of faces out there in the congregation and just marveling at how they careen in every week carrying the loads they carry—the broken-hearted and the fearful and the poor in spirit and all of them. Knowing what we know about the pain of the "perps," we would make terrible judges.

But you know who we are? We are the ones called to witness the little tornadoes in so many lives on so many days and the ones in the middle of the tornadoes that get kicked up in congregations. I wish I could say something that is worthy of blessing and honoring any clergy who may read this little essay. But all I can say is just God love you. God bless those of you who have hung, do hang, will hang in there in the Body of Christ. Thank you for trusting the Spirit to blow the tornado in the right direction and to set down the Body in the green pastures. That is faith and that is witness.

For that is the job of tornado watchers, we witness. That's all—we witness. And we have faith that God's power is made perfect in our weakness in the face of the storms. I remember being scheduled to write a sermon last year, actually for the diocesan clergy renewal of vows and instead on that day when I was supposed to think about renewing vows and the glories of being ordained, instead I witnessed a family lose the wife, the mother, after thirteen years of ravaging kidney disease. I witnessed nurses coming up from other stations around the hospital to say it had been an honor to care for her over the years. I witnessed the brother and the sister clinging to each other the way we pray our kids will cling together in the tornadoes of life. I witnessed the husband claim the authentic and loving relief of having run the race faithfully and now he can rest. I witnessed the power of the Lord made perfect in human frailty. And the rock of her death thrown into the pond of eternity that day will circle out forever and ever. For the glory of the Lord was revealed.

I don't know what I thought ordained life was going to be. I think I thought I would turn into another, much better person, which hasn't happened. I didn't know I would turn into me. I didn't know that the tornadoes of that first night were nothing compared with the howling winds I would hear down through the years. I did not know how little I could change things. I did not know how even littler that impotence matters, for our faith really is made perfect in our weakness. And isn't that something?

For Your Reflection

What do you wish the ordained people in your life knew?

If you are ordained, what do you wish the other people in your life knew?

What tornadoes are you witnessing right now?

Wrestling toward Home

Jacob was left alone; and a man wrestled with him until daybreak.

GENESIS 32:24

WHAT HAPPENS IN THE NIGHT? Perhaps we engage with the one we love. We connect in the mystery of lovemaking and then drowse and sink down into the mystery of slumber. On what we think of as the good nights, we sleep peacefully, perhaps with a little dreaming. Isn't it lovely to dream a good dream?

Jacob, for instance, had a great dream on the journey outward after he had stolen the birthright from his older brother by receiving his father's blessing in return for some fast food, which was really a terrible thing to do. And then he had to run like a wild man from the wrath of everybody but his conniving, doting mama. And yet the grasping trickster, running away from home on the road in the night, was the one to whom God gave a magnificent dream, the first dream recorded in the Bible. Isn't that something? The thief of the blessing also got the dream.

The Holy has such bad taste.

Back to his dream. It was a deeply religious dream since the word religion comes from "religare," the Latin meaning to retie or rebind. Thus religion points to reconnecting that which should never have been separated. And so Jacob dreamed of a ladder reconnecting heaven and earth, and the angels of God were ascending and descending on it. And the Lord stood beside him, the thief of birthrights and blessings who grasped at everything, including his brother's heel as he came out of the womb, and yet the Lord loved him and said, All the families of the earth shall be blessed in you and in your offspring. And Jacob woke from his sleep and the good sweet dream and said, Surely the Lord is in this place—and I did not know it! And he had the grace to be afraid.

That is what happened in the night to the young man, Jacob. God gave him a dream, a possibility, a promise, and it all happened in the dark of the night.

And then another vision, this time, twenty years later, and Jacob is a middle-aged man on another night. This time heading home, heading back with all he has accumulated—and it's a lot. Jacob had grasped and struggled and wrestled to get the most he could. And he did, in fact, get the most toys, as the bumper sticker says. And now he is ready to go home.

And isn't it something, that is what he wanted all the time— home. That's what all the wife-marrying (which he did at relatively the same time, while in our day we tend to wife-marry sequentially) and goat breeding and lambing and acquiring, and grabbing and grasping and wrestling, even when he was yet in his mother's womb, was all about. All the time he was wrestling toward home. Which at the end of the day is what I believe we all yearn for and wrestle for—home.

And so Jacob wrestled—in some good and not-so-good ways— for home. And the Lord loved him—scheming old wrestler that he was—and blessed him all along the way, but now he is almost there and he is anxious. He is a wreck, and he should be, what with the broken-hearted, abandoned father and the cheated brother waiting (well, not really waiting—the brother is on his way in a cloud of dust with a small army). And so Jacob sends his family and his flocks along to safety, and then he waits alone in the night for the struggle.

In the *Genesis* series on PBS Bill Moyers asked my Old Testament teacher, Walter Brueggemann, "Why do you suppose it is that the night time is the time when you struggle?" Brueggemann replied, "Because I am too damn good at daytime work."

That is why we wrestle in the night; we are too damn good at the daytime work. Jacob and you and me—that is why we wrestle in the night.

Of course there are those who don't wrestle enough.

The following scenario has repeated itself too often in the last years. Two men come with backpacks into a little café in the supposedly safe zone of a city in the broad daylight. They sit together and drink tea for half an hour or so. One of them, according to witnesses, appears to reassure his more nervous colleague. And then one gets up and leaves and a moment later an explosion is heard and then the man left behind in the café blows himself up as well. And between the two of them, they kill of course themselves and ten other people. No words had been spoken to the other patrons, no arguing, no wrestling—just boom . . . boom.

For a moment, can we imagine that those two men had engaged with the people around them, maybe argued with them really loudly and struggled long and hard with their rage in this bitter time in the Middle East? What if those people had been willing to wrestle, to connect in the mystery no one of us can control? For at the end of the day, the biggest things in human lives—families, homes, faiths, native lands—are worth wrestling for, since the alternative to wrestling in grave conflict is mutual annihilation.

Wrestling is not easy. It is intimate and disturbing, even terrifying, even for the old wrestler Jacob, who, it turns out of course, was wrestling with the Holy. And you know what that means? He embraced the Holy—all night long—the Holy and the man embraced. So in the struggle was communion.

And at the end of the wrestling, it was a hard night, but it was a good night. And Jacob was truly blessed—his own earned blessing this time. And he left the struggle a changed man, with a new name, Israel, and a new blessing, his own, and, too, a permanent limp. For we do not wrestle with the Holy without cost. Jacob wrestled, he embraced, and now he will limp all his days, a marked man, through with wrestling, ready for home.

For Your Reflection

When it comes to the big things, when it comes to the Holy— are you willing to wrestle?

What is worth wrestling for?

With whom do you wrestle?

Where is God in the match?

In Your Own Backyard

*For we know that the whole creation has been groaning together
in the pangs of childbirth. . . .*

ROMANS 8:22

*When the mountains are overthrown and the seas uplifted, the
universe at Florissant flings itself against a gnat and preserves it.*

Dr. Arthur C. Peale, Hayden Expedition Geologist, 1873

WE HAD DRIVEN BY HER LITTLE HOUSE on a mountain road between Denver and Colorado Springs and noticed the handwritten sign out front: Fossils.

I said, Oh let's stop, and my husband, having been weakened by the thin mountain air, actually said okay and pulled into the driveway up to the garage, now half fossil shop.

We walked into a small whitewashed room and she met us coming from an interior door connecting the house to the shop and we all smiled hello, how are you. She was lovely in a gentle, faded way, very neatly dressed with a tucked-in shirt over worn blue jeans and sneakers. Her eyes matched the jeans and her face had a pleasing stillness.

She had an unusual accent because it turns out that she was from Denmark by way of New Jersey but had lived in Colorado for twenty-five years. You could hear the layers of the lands and the peoples in her voice.

We asked if we could look around, which actually meant looking right in front of us at the only thing in the room, a small clean
two-shelved case. She smiled, of course, and floated back as if to
give us more freedom and light to explore.

The case contained, oh, maybe forty pieces of earth about the
size of various cookies. You had to really look hard at each one for
the fossil images were imprinted most often in the same color as
the surrounding material. But when you did look, you saw hints of
ferns, pieces of insects, whole leaves and seeds, and those lovely
spiral things. I asked her where she got them. And she said, In the
backyard. Really? we said.

For twenty-five years she had been mining her backyard for fossils, since the same fossil-rich ancient lake bed that forms the
Florissant National Monument stretches across her little piece of
property.

I asked her does she do this mining every day and she said, Oh
no. Just when I need to restock. And then she smiled the smile of
someone who has enough and knows that she has enough, and the
peace of that showing in her eyes.

We admired this one and that one and finally picked out what
I thought were a pair of maple seeds but later understood are the
same maple seed cloven in two so each fossil is the mirror image of
the other. When I hold the two pieces together, there is the one
seed—the oneness—that floated down into a lovely lake thirty-four
million years ago.

Had you been there, at the long-ago time, you might have
said—but you weren't there, I am sure, because this was the time
before us, though after dinosaurs—but if you had been there, you
would have thought Oh, that seed is wasted because it missed the
earth and went into the deep water. That seed did not accomplish
the creative purpose for which it was made. For maple seeds don't
sprout at the bottom of very deep lakes. And so it must be wasted.

And then thirty-four million years go by—just the twinkling of the eye of God—and a woman from Denmark who grew up in New Jersey moves to Colorado in search of what life I do not know, but she had the look of a seeker who had found. And the woman digs around in her own backyard and finds a chunk of shale and splits it open and there is the cloven maple seed. And—just guessing here—she probably smiles. And then she puts her find in her clean and plain little display case for some tourists from Tennessee to take the one seed, now split wide open, back to their home in the shadows of the Appalachians, the oldest mountains in the world.

And the woman in the Tennessee cabin—me—every once in a while gets them out and studies the fossil twins—two little chunks of what looks like cardboard that has been very wet and swelled up so that the layers slightly separated and then dried stuck together. Toward the edge of one chunk is what appears to be a very large sperm or a tiny tadpole. Its twin is wiggling in the opposite direction on the other chunk. And I think about its life so many ages ago in the prehistoric, prehuman, postdinosaur hardwood forest on the edge of the lush meadows near the mountain that erupted and poured out the lava that sunk to the bottom of the lake and preserved this little voyager. And how it has been there, part of the creation, though hidden and quiescent, all these ages, and now I enjoy it and protect it from our cat, who is a much bigger threat than a volcano since he evidently likes to play soccer with fossils.

And then I look out my window at the hardwood forests all around our place, which are pre-the-future and post-the-past— but not really. And I sense my self in this very moment surrounded by the uplifted eons-ancient and ever-new green and shaley mountains and the hollers between. And I hear the creek running full and loud. And I remember the April flights on our mountain—of billions of maple tree seeds with their translucent single-wing sails and I smile. And the maple seed and the tadpole and the sperm all fill me with wonder at the audacity of their journeys—wriggles and floats and sinkings and all.

Just for the moment, I glimpse the potential that was there so many millions of years ago, is now, and will be forever. It stirs my soul. And for the moment, I lift up out of my own wrigglings and strivings and sinkings and failings and I get it. Nothing is wasted. That which does not sprout in this eon may in the next in a whole new way.

We paid her and she wished us a good journey and wrapped up the twin chunks of the maple seed in a package very carefully because she said it has to travel.

Isn't that the truth?

For Your Reflection

What are the layers of lands and peoples in your voice?

Are there seeds in your life that you believe are wasted?

Could you be taking the short view?

Westminster Drive

On this mountain the LORD of Hosts will make for all peoples a
feast of rich food, a feast of well-aged wines . . . strained clear.

ISAIAH 25:6

I GREW UP WITH FORMIDABLE little old ladies so I was surprised
by my nervousness on the day I was to meet some of the same
species who were relatives of my intended intended. A point of
clarification—I call him my intended intended because on that
spring afternoon in 1969, he had not declared his intentions. I, on
the other hand, intended to be his intended, if you know what I
mean. And I thought this visit to his grandmother and his aunt was
a good sign. Of his intentions.

We settled in on their front porch—sitting on indestructible—
actually un-killable and hideous beyond description—rattan furniture, which in the decades since has traveled through a number of
cousinly abodes all the way to our screen porch up in the mountains
of East Tennessee. The cushions are hard as rocks, and the frames
will outlive us, too, but how do you ditch even upholstered aged
members of the family? I am ahead of myself.

Back to 1969 and Westminster Drive, when I am sitting on the
stuff for the first time, and we are all smiling and nodding like you
do. We are still cooing about how warm the spring weather is and
how good to see and meet and all and all, and then Sue Brown the
Younger pipes up and says, We have a refreshing new aperitif to

offer you. At least new to mama and me, she says modestly. We hope you'll enjoy, so cool and light on a warm afternoon.

We smile timidly and offer our appreciation, though in retrospect I believe my intended looked a little alarmed as his aunt disappeared into the house. You see, he's been here before. And no wonder he wonders what she will show up with, for in fact she returns in just no time with a whacking fifth of something called Thunderbird, which, if you're unfamiliar with the vineyard, resides on the shelf of the convenience store right behind the cash register up next to the Ripple. But here it is—chilled—on Westminster Drive on a silver tray of course with cunning little cut-glass stemware tinkling as she walks, her little heels clicking, and her face beaming as she moves toward us offering the gift.

She asks if we are familiar with the vintner, and Carroll says, Why yes, he'd seen Thunderbird before but never had the lucky chance to actually partake. And Grandmother chimes in and says a friend had suggested it and I have since figured out it must have been one of her friends at the alcohol treatment house where she played cards with the residents every late Thursday afternoon for years and years until, to get her to retire in her nineties, they had to give her a huge going-away party.

Can't you just see them at the card table? The tiny crooked-backed very old lady and the shaky brokenhearted men. Two clubs, three hearts, pass—and then somebody sighs and says, well, I sure miss that old Thunderbird. So let me just get us some more lemonade. How about you, Mrs. Sterne? And she smiles inquiringly . . . Thunderbird?

And the rest is history. So I sat for the first time on the hideous rattan but oh not for the last. And I sipped the Thunderbird—pink, sweet, nasty beyond words—and I ate a cookie that had seen better days. I realized at that point that these are not food people and my people in Mississippi and Louisiana are food people. But I think—looking back—I think I thought this may be home. I think here I might find myself at home. Or perhaps I just intended to find myself at home, which I believe is the faith response that gets us the most mileage in this old world.

For Your Reflection

Where do you find yourself surprisingly at home?
What are marks of hospitality for you?

Omaha Beach and Scripture

*Moses to the Children of Israel: You shall put these words of
mine in your heart and soul. . . . Teach them to your children,
talking about them when you are home and when you are away,
when you lie down and when you rise.*

DEUTERONOMY 11:18–19

MY HUSBAND AND I WENT TO Omaha Beach where the Americans
landed on D-Day. The morning was timeless—the sky gray and low,
billowed, still—so that we were enclosed in a small gray world of
breakers and beach and cliffs looming over the beach. A few seagulls
wheeling. Peaceful. The beach has always been my idea of peaceful.

You know, don't you, that on Omaha Beach, nothing went right
on that other cloudy spring morning so many years ago. Nothing.
The armored tanks had sunk in the channel crossing. Hardly anybody landed where they were supposed to with tidal currents and
the wind pushing them sideways. The waters were mined so that
here and there while still in the sea—exploding fountains of body
parts and metal. The men were nauseated, cold, exhausted already,
huddling in the bottom of each landing craft. I do not believe they
wasted their time arguing about hell and heaven or throwing Bible
quotes at each other. Surely instead they were hard praying, each to
the God of his understanding.

But then the landing craft door would drop open and those
people did what they were trained and trained and trained to do so
that all the words of training became flesh and deed. One by one

they did it—they clambered out—guns lifted over the waves—all
that gear and their boots—falling forward into the water half-swim-
ming, sinking, drowning, falling, crawling onto the beach and all the
time the death raining down from the cliffs—fifteen hundred feet to
get to the base of the cliffs—the guns aimed at you, thousands of
mines in the sand, not knowing where to step, watching the buddy
next to you explode. As the morning screamed on, there was so much
wreckage in the water that the landings had to stop and they were on
their own. But they were trained and they knew what to do. In that
small hellish world of breakers and beach and cliffs, they knew the
right action, in spite of the death and the chaos, and they did it.

It is truly beyond my comprehension—the camaraderie, the
courage, the sacrifice—of D-Day. They just kept throwing themselves on those beaches, dying and coming and coming on and
dying and just keeping on and on, really winning the day by the
sheer immensity of the sacrifice—so many thousands and thousands dead. But the evil was so clear. The cost so necessary. And the
prize of freedom and peace so dear.

Carroll and I saw them at rest in the American cemetery in
Normandy—white marble crosses and stars of David as far as the
eye can see, lined up this way, that way, this way—all that pristine
order and beauty and symmetry and completion where had been
so much pain, so much blood, so much dying. I will carry with me
for the rest of my life the agonizing paradox of the pristine order
and beauty of the military dead.

There are very few gifts that great evil has to offer, but one
potential gift is that great evil clarifies the situation and gives us the
chance to respond with nobility and sacrifice. In our day, with so
much complexity and ambiguity, so much information and disin-
formation—how do we respond with nobility and sacrifice? Even
the military—where discipline and hierarchy and clarity of purpose
and ethic are a way of life—even the military is in a foggy new day,
battling stateless, uniformless armies led by shadowy figures. Where

is the battlefield? Who is the enemy? What are the ethical boundaries of dealing with prisoners? With suicide as a major tactic, how do you deal with people who are willing to purposefully kill themselves?

If the military is in a new day of fog and chaos, is it any wonder that the rest of us are? Really the only ones beyond struggle and chaos and the challenge of how to live a noble life are the dead in the gleaming white rows, may they rest in peace. And may we learn from them some strategies for noble action in the strange challenges of our own day.

We may be living in chaotic times, but we still want to live meaningful, even noble lives. To do that we need, as did those soldiers, the power of discipline through training and habit. Moses talked about this when he said to the people—don't slip and slide and whine and petty-stuff your way through life. Accept discipline. Accept training—make time and space for that which matters in your heart and soul. Learn the depths and habits of the holy words: Faith, Love, Sacrifice, Courage, Hope. Teach them to your children. Talk about them when you are home and away. When you lie down and when you rise. The call to discipline by Moses is the same call to discipline as the military and also the same call to discipline as the nonviolent civil rights movement and also the same call to discipline as AA. And for Christians, Jesus makes the same call, to live as people of discipline, as disciples of the larger life of faith, courage, sacrifice, love, hope.

One of the primary training tools for people of the Christian persuasion is the reading and study of Scripture because when you study Scripture the doors fling open to nobility in every area of human striving. It would be really good news if we who are trying to follow Christ would not just criticize those who make an idol out of the Bible but also avail ourselves of the riches therein. To pray Scripture (for me this means reading and resting in Scripture preferably with a small group of seekers) lights the way toward being the people God created us to be. This Scripture habit does not help us find the simple answers, for it is my experience that when we read Scripture beyond our favorite little bits that we have already picked out to bolster our opinions, then we know there are no simple answers.

For instance, I no longer discuss the book of Leviticus with people who insist on championing its literal moral directives unless they have sacrificed a goat in the last few weeks. Of course, if you have sacrificed a goat lately, then maybe we need to talk about more than sexual morality.

Instead of grabbing a piece of Scripture and holding on for dear life, what if you discipline yourself to adventure into Scripture in all its complexity, for then you are led to read the newspaper more deeply than the headlines and your neighbor's words more deeply than the idle chatter and you read your own heart with more clarity, even with all its shadows and ambiguity.

Scripture comes to life in faith communities who take seriously the mission to train us how to talk about the important stuff and how to listen to each other and encourage each other to live gratefully and nobly with faith, sacrifice, love, courage, hope. To me, it is just too hard to know how to even point yourself toward a noble life without a community.

I believe that the grace of God is the most powerful reality in the universe. But I also believe that we need the discipline and training of a Scripture-savvy faith community to show us how to get into the water, run the beaches, and climb the cliffs.

For Your Reflection

What do you know and not know of Scripture?

Knowing that one eats an elephant one bite at a time, how can you invigorate your study of Scripture?

Who has taught you about living a noble life?

Angels Unawares and
Demons Unawarer

Be not forgetful to entertain strangers; for thereby some
have entertained angels unawares.

HEBREW 13:2 (KJV)

WHEN I WAS A CHILD, the Presbyterians, or just my grandmother, or somebody must have taught me the verse out of the King James Bible that starts "Be not forgetful to entertain strangers," just like the more contemporary versions, but ends with the haunting invitation "for thereby some have entertained angels unawares."

I thought about them a lot. The unaware angels. Were they just not alert, those angels? Were they sleepy or daydreamers or confused from the cloud-floating? Or—and this was the most interesting possibility—maybe angels were lost from heaven and wandering around on the earth, maybe right outside Power Elementary, and maybe I would be the one to see their wings dragging in the dust and say, Hey, excuse me, are you aware that you are an angel and your wings are dragging?

What would you do to entertain angels once they were more or less aware? Back then, I thought chocolate pudding might work. They might like that. Perhaps they would want to play some harps, though I hoped not. Mainly, though, I thought about how do you know an unaware angel when you see one and what do you do with them when you get one?

I think this angel business still needs our attention because our better angels need our help. It is hard to be a self-respecting angel these days, so I think they have gotten apathetic. Show me an apathetic angel and I will show you an angel unaware. Their malaise may be because angels have been dumbed down and sweetly gooeyed up. This is, I believe, probably very disturbing to honest-to-God angels who never claimed to be sweet or, well, angelic. Real angels are fierce and ruthlessly committed to carrying the messages of their Maker. Look at Gabriel and Michael and all; they were swashbucklers. They did not just show up and be sweet; they passed on big news, since after all the word "angel" comes from *angelos*, which means "messenger." These guys are the Pony Express of creation, not lapdogs.

So the real job of angels is to pass hard and living good news on. Sometimes they show up in a conversation or in a dream or in a moment on a bus or most often for me in the checkout line at the grocery store. They are more likely to stir up the spirit than to smooth things down. Angels can be downright irritating since angels are in the business of startling people with the Holy and thus jump-starting people to come alive in the Spirit.

Today in every church—really every community—there are angels unawares. They are often wasting their time and their people's time talking about stuff that does not bring good news. The aware angels very rarely pass on gossip, for instance. Instead, the real honest-to-God aware angels almost always are on a message that is pointed directly at the person entertaining the angel. Gabriel didn't show up and tell Mary that her neighbor was having an affair or that the music in the synagogue needed spiffing up and Mary should complain about it. Gabriel showed up and said Mary, Hail. The Lord is with you. The Holy Spirit will come upon you. And the rest is his story.

And of course there are also demons unawares as well. Unlike our better angels, the demonic ones thrive on unawareness. The most dangerous demons I know are the nasty-nice ones who are totally unaware of the damage they do. And thus demon recognition is what Jesus did so often with miserable people. He named the demons and called the demons out. In our day, we are scared to say boo to demons for fear of offending someone, and so the demons of self-absorption and bigotry and pride and envy and greed and fear and all the others get by with soul murder.

Whether we want to be or not, we are all in the Angel Entertaining and Awareness Business as well as the Demon Recognition Program. Since sometimes the demon and the angel are one and the same (see Satan working on Job), it is tricky business and takes us helping each other sort out the good news from the mischief.

Some of our most important angel and demon work needs to happen with the ones of whom we ourselves, who are so often strangers to ourselves, are least aware. Are you aware of the angels and demons, muttering or fluttering, in your very own soul?

For Your Reflection

Do you know an angel unawares? Who?

What are your thoughts on an angel awareness and demon recognition program in your soul?

How do we rely more on our better angels in communities of faith?

The Vine

I am the vine, you are the branches. Those who abide in me and I in them bear much fruit, because apart from me you can do nothing. Whoever does not abide in me is thrown away like a branch and withers. . . . If you abide in me, and my words abide in you, ask for whatever you wish, and it will be done for you.

JOHN 15:5–7

GROWING UP IN SEMITROPICAL Mississippi taught me early on to love and yet be wary of vines. There were wonderful vines—confederate jasmine—dark-gloss green leaves, waxy white blooms, crawling up the side of our front gallery to my bedroom. I dreamed in jasmine for years. And cucumbers and melons and tomato vines ripening in the hot sun. And honeysuckle smelling just like school is out and when you picked the little petal-spraddled bloom and pulled one of the stamens with the tiny ball on the end—you got a sweet dollop of nectar right on your tongue. And the sweetness was primeval—straight from as Gerard Manley Hopkins calls it—*the dearest freshness deep down things.*

Honeysuckle however wasn't allowed on the ancient picket fences around my grandfather's house. It would have pulled them down. You've got to watch some vines or they will take over your life. Shall we say the magic word—kudzu?

Vines are wonderful but they can be serious troublemakers. A tree you can count on to stay where it is supposed to. A bush, a flower the same—though invasives sometimes need to be disciplined. But a vine by its very nature is going where you do not know, twisting and turning and reaching and growing—not because a seed was planted or a root reached out to throw up a different shoot but because the whole vine is surging with life and has this dearest, dangerous freshness deep down in it—abiding in it, life in it abiding and yet always on the move.

So I think Jesus chose this way of telling us who he is on purpose. If you want a solid, humdrum, no surprise life, then stay away from him. He is the vine and he is dangerous. He will trouble your life—and if he isn't troubling our values and our assumptions then we are disconnected. This is true of individuals and it is true of churches. For if the life of Jesus is surging through you, you are no longer in control—either as a person or a community—and so if the life of Jesus is surging through us then no telling how he will grow and change us.

Remember he didn't say I am the tree of life—which stays put and we stand under its shade and then walk away and do our thing. And he didn't say I am the fragile flower of life, which blooms for a season for us to maybe take into our homes or the church and then toss. What he said is I am the vine and you are the branches. Your very next turn, your very next choice, our very existence— each of us, all of us—comes through the holy vine, when we are connected. Or not if we are cut off. Which is the literal definition of sin.

We are not invited to admire Jesus on Sunday and walk through our week cut loose—that is to live shallow and die, really. We are invited instead to trust and to know that we can abide and live in the vine that gives us direction and meaning and power. And so sometimes you are in a season of winter when nothing looks like it's happening. And yet you abide. And sometimes you are in a season of confusing growth and lack of direction and yet you abide.

And sometimes you get twisted around a situation you would have never chosen and yet you abide. And sometimes you get pruned back—and let's face it we all would prefer to do our own pruning, but we can't—and so even in the pruning we abide. We are not the ultimate creators and shapers of our own lives. There is this unknowable Pruner, Shaper, Creator, God even beyond Jesus.

And so, there is this, I believe, unknowable life of God that Jesus always, always pointed to and lived out of and died into and rose from the dead through and so Jesus says I am connected to the Source and you are through me—and we abide in the dearest freshness deep down things—all things in Christ.

And so—you are not the vine. I am not the vine. Our communities of faith are not the vine. The Bible is not the vine. We are the branches. We cannot do our own pruning, much less prune anybody else. And we do not cause our growth. And even the one who is the Vine, Christ Jesus in whom we abide, kept pointing beyond himself to the Life beyond all creeds and temples and vines and vineyards. And he kept saying, listen I abide in God. And you abide in me and watch what happens.

It is true. Vines can be dangerous to our structures, our values, the way we make sense of our lives. I remember this as I picture the ivy on the front wall of our church. We have cut the ivy off the other walls of the church because it clings and messes up the mortar between the bricks and wants to get in the windows. Eventually in the decades to come we may have to pull all of it down but there on the front we leave it for now—for the beauty and for the truth—that we are part of that which is growing, we are part of the vine that goes where we do not know and sometimes where we do not want, and that from time to time we need to be reminded that God is reaching reaching reaching toward us through every wall we erect into the very heart of us—reaching reaching through all the barriers we throw up to protect ourselves.

It is easy to talk this abiding in the vine talk and it is so hard for us to trust and to submit to live on the vine, which means to love the living vine more than the structure that supports it. To live connected to the One who made us and to each other. And yet it is the only way to real life—to breathe and trust and submit to live as a branch of the vine. For there is the dearest freshness deep down in your life and mine. And Jesus makes the wild promise that if we abide there we will receive every desire of our deepest heart. This is not magic or hucksterism. This is the mystery of Christ. Abide in the vine and ask for whatever and it will be done.

For Your Reflection

Where is the vine growing fresh in your life?
What are you tempted to mistake as the vine?
How are you abiding in the vine? How are you cut loose?

A Pro's Final Gig

If we live, we live to the Lord, and if we die, we die to the Lord;
so then, whether we live or whether we die, we are the Lord's.

ROMANS 14:8

SHE WAS IN THE BED by the window. Asleep, I think. On second glance, maybe asleep. Maybe playing possum.

I had been meaning to get by to see her for about six months. Since she was almost a hundred years old, delay could be problematic. But I had done the little calculation I do in my head about the boundaries of appropriate pastoral care, which in my case turn out to be so much more restrictive and self-protective than the Good Samaritan's portfolio. I bet the Good Samaritan never checked to see if the half-dead guy in the ditch was on the parish rolls.

So anyway. I went to see her because an eighty-five-year-old mutual friend had asked me to, since she was an Episcopalian who had been moved into our county by her family. I took my time going to see her because she wasn't a parishioner and she was advertised as a "difficult person." Pastoral care calculus: supposedly Episcopalian . . . ornery. It took me six months to get there.

She opens one eye. Sees stranger, clerical collar, woman—potentially an off-putting combination. I smile and ask her if she is so-and-so and tell her that I am from the local parish and that I had heard she was Episcopalian. She barks back—and Catholic and Presbyterian—nothing wrong with my religion! Not a thing.

I stammer that oh I didn't think there was. She glares. I wilt. I am going into my one minute and outta-here mode. Then out of the blue, she said I worked for three federal judges, loved one of them like a son, raised him. I said really?

And then she said it's real different here. All these women. I have never worked around so many women. I am realizing that she sees this nursing home gig as a job. And it is.

I try to think of something to say back that is politically correct about being around all women but unfortunately, at that very moment, at work, we are in one of those tiresome, tiny church squabbles involving buckets of women of a certain age including myself.

I abandon political correctness. I find I have perked up. I say I work with a lot of women. She says, well, just ignore spats and they go away. Don't give little prissy fusses any attention and they starve.

My erstwhile feminist heart quavers. What on earth am I doing putting down women with a ninety-eight-year-old woman? Well, it quavers briefly. And then I say, well, it is tiring. I get sucked into the petty stuff all the time. She grimaces and says you must like it or you wouldn't.

Ouch. I change the subject. Tell me about the judges. She does. Especially the young one that she "raised." She told me that sometimes she just wanted to find a ladder and climb into her third-story office without having to chitchat her way through all the courthouse crowd. This is remarkable. I know exactly what she is talking about; however, my office is on the ground floor and all I would need to do is unlatch the window. This has possibilities.

She retired at sixty-nine, although they asked her to stay to seventy. She told them I can't stand one more year of you and you can't stand one more year of me. I ask what she did when she quit work and she sweeps her hand around the walls of the room where there are delicate watercolors of birds in flight. She loves birds. I tell her about another resident of this nursing home—dead now—who could stand so still that the birds ate out of her hands and that anybody could if you stood still long enough. She snorts. No way.

She says her daughter lives in the next county and visits, though she is busy with grandchildren. She says I don't blame her; I was busy, too. Another daughter only calls when she wants something; she can tell that it is that daughter by the way the phone rings. I say you are kidding. She says oh no I am not. And even with the closer daughter, she says, when she comes in the room, I steel myself. She thinks she's going to fix me.

I ask her what she does all day now. And she says she thinks about God all the time. All the time. I say what do you think. And she says Indescribable. We sit.

After a while it's time. I ask her if she wants someone to bring communion and she says yes. I ask her if I can come back. Yes. I leave. A witness.

For Your Reflection

Who do you know who is a "pro" at living?

What do you want from those who love you when you need help?

What is your gift to your workplace?

Beyond Opinion

Early on the first day of the week, while it was still dark . . .

JOHN 20:1

I AM ALWAYS AMAZED at how a group of people—or even just three people or even just two people or even just one person over time—can see the same thing, hear the same thing, experience the same thing, and come away with totally different opinions as to what just happened. This is one of the most constant—sometimes hilarious, sometimes frustrating—experiences of my life as a priest and as a family member and a friend.

So I will go through some liturgy and see just where I messed something up and then someone will say, Wow, that worship really touched me to my soul. Or I will be in a meeting and think, goodness, we are all such geniuses and that was such a good conversation and we got so much done, and someone else will say, We seemed so lost and addled.

Or my son and his wife have just bought a little house in an Atlanta in-town neighborhood and they see fascinating, diverse neighbors and a cottage garden coming and their grandmother sees weeds and motorcycle gangs and crack houses.

Or people see someone on life support due to an unfixable injury or illness, and some have the opinion that this is a person trapped in a body waiting to be freed for new life. And others have the opinion that this is a helpless victim who needs to be protected from those who would kill her and take away any possibility of life. And on and on it goes, the opinion machine.

In the most popular blood sport of our day, breathless reporters line up dueling experts in the great grope of opinion makers and opinion evaluators and again and again they all meet to do battle at some courthouse somewhere over some new/old issue *du jour* with everybody sticking a mike in everybody else's face to get their latest opinion on someone else's latest opinion. Because that is what we do in our day. We have lots of opinions and we hold onto them as if our life and the world and God's truth depend on us defending our opinions to the death.

There is another way. Which is the Easter way, which is to give up on one's opinion as the fortress of life and give way to trust in the One beyond opinion. And so the Easter way is to at least begin to trust and reach shyly or desperately or joyfully out far beyond your little opinion, to reach for the transforming, ever-healing, ever-moving mystery of the power of God.

There is precedent. In the Gospel of John the writer says three people went to go check on the tomb and each of them had a different reaction. Mary Magdalene thought his body had been stolen, which is what I would have thought. Peter ran all the way into the tomb and stood there speechless and confused and, as usual with him, just didn't know what to think. And the third, the disciple whom Jesus loved (who by the way was probably the one who told this version to the guy who wrote it down two generations later, but even sixty years later it comes through loud and clear, like a lot of us, he thinks he is the beloved). At any rate, the disciple who thinks that Jesus loves him best runs like a madman to get there and then can't even go in and hangs outside the tomb, appalled.

And they were all three of them afraid and did not know what had happened and just were there—helpless and without really a firm opinion on the empty tomb at all. And thank God. Thank

God they did not just grab an opinion and hang on for dear life. And they were the ones who were there.

It is no coincidence that we have four different gospels with different resurrection accounts and even just in this one gospel we have three people reacting differently, authentically, faithfully, and so remaining open to the transformation of despair to hope and the resurrection of death to life. It is so good that they are different one from another because that is the God-given truth. We all see things differently for we are all unique and our uniqueness is from God. And what matters is not the opinions about, but our openness to the reality of, in Tillich's splendid phrase, *New Being*.

Thank God they didn't just form an opinion and stop there. They would never have seen the resurrected Jesus as they all eventually did. And they are our teachers and help us remember that Christ is let loose in the world to be and do and love and heal who knows where, when, how, who. So that when we remember them we can let go of our little opinions and reach out for God and trust that God will be there reaching back.

Maybe, like Mary Magdalene, you are in a place where God seems to have been stolen away. Or maybe, like Peter, you are in a place where you are just confused and baffled as to whether God is in your life or your life is just an empty tomb. Or maybe, like the beloved disciple—that's his story and he's sticking to it—you are in a place where you just see and believe and trust that God is there for you even around tombs, even when it's impossible to have any old opinion on what is next.

No matter where you are, your life can be so much richer than opinion. May your life be one of insight, of depth, of yes, seeing what you see and authentically trying to make sense of that, but not stopping there as if what you see is God's only truth. And may all our lives be lives of not mouthing opinions, but lives of seeing a bit more, trusting a bit deeper, and being beckoned by grace to

trust and believe that Jesus is alive and loose in the world—transforming each of us and all of us into eternity. Because Alleluia,
Christ is risen. The Lord is risen indeed, alleluia.

For Your Reflection

When does opinion just not matter?

Where do you see yourself and your community struggling to
move beyond mouthing opinions?

What would you have thought if you had arrived at the empty
tomb?

The One Thing

Martha, Martha, you are worried and distracted by
many things; there is need of only one thing.

LUKE 10:41–42

I REMEMBER AN ACQUAINTANCE of the family, named Ethelbelle, who happened to travel a great deal with her husband, and they would stay in very fancy places all over the world. And Ethelbelle would get into the hotel room, wherever it was—the Crillon in Paris, the Ritz in London, the Plaza in New York—and no matter what time of day or night, she would kick off her shoes and pick up the phone and call room service to order a chicken salad sandwich. First thing every time, wherever she was.

And then she would wait for the staff to bring the chicken salad sandwich and see how that went—the time it took for delivery, the style and manners of the server, the presentation on the plate. And then, of course, she would eat the chicken salad sandwich and see how that went. And then she would weigh the pros and cons and evaluate and make up her mind and then tell the long-suffering husband (whose name totally escapes me) whether the hotel, and thus the trip and thus her life at that particular moment was satisfactory. Because of that one thing—the chicken salad sandwich.

And so through that one thing, the chicken salad sandwich, she made sense of her journeys through the world. This single focus brings a sort of clarity and peace in and of itself, does it not? It would be so soothing to have one criterion—one thing—determine whether a relationship is okay or not, the job is okay or not, the country is okay or not, the church is okay or not, or whatever is okay or not, including me, including you. I mean, that is efficient isn't it? Check out the chicken salad sandwich—and boom, go from there. It calms your mind to know the one thing when you see it, and sometimes it's even more satisfying to know the one thing that you don't see and then be able to reject what may be a tiresomely complex situation quickly and neatly. You don't find the good chicken salad sandwich? You're outta there.

After all, even Jesus says, to the worried and distracted Martha, Honey, you are worrying about too many things. There is need of only one thing.

But it is just . . . well, what is the one thing?

I don't know how to name the one thing I need, much less the one thing you need. I really don't have that one word for our yearning. Though I am beginning to believe that yearning is the great human leveler—we all yearn—and I wonder if we don't yearn for the same one thing. I wonder if we share the deepest yearning in common, though we cannot recognize each other's yearning as our own.

But oh, do I recognize the frenzy that distracts and worries us and sends us frantic to find just something to hang onto in the chaos of our days. Here are words of Thomas Merton (*Conjectures of a Guilty Bystander*) for we frenzied people who yearn for the one thing:

> The rush and pressure of modern life are a form, perhaps the most common form, of its innate violence. . . . Frenzy destroys our inner capacity for peace. It destroys the fruitfulness of our work because it kills the root of inner wisdom which makes work fruitful.

Even in our searches for the one thing, we are a frenzied, frenzied culture. Running here and there, frenzied for our security, frenzied for the well-being of our children, frenzied on the job, frenzied in politics, polling ourselves hour by hour rather than trying to grasp the complexity of the life-and-death issues that face us. We are a frenzied people in frenzied families in a frenzied culture in a frenzied world, and too often we try to solve that with simplemindedness: black/white, bad/good, acceptable chicken salad/unacceptable chicken salad.

And so we are always declaring up or down, yes or no, to little chicken stuff, though we know down deep there is more. Surely there is something more than any or all of the things in the universe that we could buy and consume, even with the best service and the most beautiful presentation and the taste of homemade mayonnaise sweet in our mouth. Surely there is more than anything we can make or taste or grasp or buy or sell. When all the time the stars declare God's glory and the mountains sing God's peace and the birds of the air flutter and float by the grace of God, what are we doing? And if the beasts large and small and all things bright and beautiful are just breathing and living and in the moment, what are we doing? The whole creation dances, except for us, for we are a frenzied people and we do not know how to be hospitable to the holy.

As a child, I thought Ethelbelle was an exotic genius, and surely she was a forerunner of our day in this chicken-salad culture when to shop for and consume the best (including religion) is the pathetic vestige we have of the search for the Holy Grail.

Okay, okay. So she probably missed the mark on the one thing. But don't you wish you could name it and judge the days accordingly and make all of your journeys make sense? It is the pathway out of the frenzy, to seek the one thing.

Jesus didn't even name it—he just said, dear ones, it's true. All you need is the one thing. That's all you need.

Now what is it?

For Your Reflection

Really, what is the one thing you need?

How can we heal ourselves of frenzy?

The One Thing—Part Two

LAST SUMMER I SPENT A MONTH away from my normal frenzy with two sisters—my mother and my aunt. From my earliest days I knew they were very different women. My mother has a plan for each day and everything in her house is in apple-pie order and she is in her church every Sunday she's in town. And at eighty-six she still has community volunteer responsibilities, particularly with the public library, plus she can beat the socks off of most anybody at any card game you want to try.

My aunt, on the other hand, is a writer and most at home in the interior world of the mind and of the beauty of stories. Things just grow around her without much effort or order. She has plants that are thirty/forty years old and that have moved without complaint from household to household with her paintings and photographs and pottery and sculpture, and creativity of all kinds that just sort of meanders through her space. She does readings and book signings occasionally, and mother goes with her some because they navigate well together—for their very differences complete one another.

And so they journey together, with and without parents and husbands and children and grandchildren, for eighty-plus years now, authentic and alive and in the moment.

My computer screen saver is a photograph from last summer in a moment with them. The late, late afternoon sun is lighting them from behind as they stand at my aunt's fence and cut some roses—the flowers deep coral and shimmering in the light. Mother is in her creamy yellow silk pantsuit already knowing just how many roses she wants and the small blue vase she will use and the table behind the sofa where the flowers will reside and who she will take some to at the nursing home tomorrow. And my aunt in sweats and tennis shoes is just enjoying the play of the light on the fence and the spilling-over beauty of the roses that she's rooted from somewhere else and of course remembering the source of the rooting. And by God's grace, for no particular reason, it was a moment of fullness for me, and whatever it is we all yearn for was there with us and among us and around us.

I don't think either one of them could tell us or would dream to tell us what the one thing is. And I am sure they are incomplete and yearning just like the rest of us. But by and large, they are not distracted; they are not frenzied; and they don't waste time on chicken salad. Well, actually they do make quite good chicken salad but always knowing its place in the universe. By and large those sisters are the people God made them to be. And somehow that makes each of them, in her own way, from moment to moment, hospitable to the holy. Just like us on our better days.

I want to point toward the still holy oneness in the midst of frenzy. And I ask God to help us to live authentically through all our days and to invite into our moments the still and holy One who brings us all to life.

For Your Reflection

Who gives you the gift of stillness?

With whom is differentness a blessing to you?

How do we make room for differentness in communities of faith?

Fairness and the God of the Forest

[T]hose eighteen who were killed when the tower of Siloam
fell on them—do you think that they were worse offenders
than all the others living in Jerusalem?

LUKE 13:4

LIKE EVERYBODY ELSE, the people around Jesus wanted to know what the deal is. Why do bad things happen to good people? And has, they ask Jesus, has God arranged the universe appropriately so that more bad things happen to bad people and more good things happen to good people? Because that would be fair.

So they ask, when the tower of Siloam fell on eighteen people, were they worse sinners than everybody else in Jerusalem? God knows we have seen too much of this question in our day. Was the woman who made it to work on time on September 11, 2001, less worthy of life than the guy who stopped to get a haircut? Or did the family who went shopping in Baghdad deserve to be obliterated more than the family down the street who decided to spend the day at home?

You know the answer. You have lived it. Sometimes the good and beautiful die young. Sometimes gentle, kind people have one ghastly thing after another happen while sleazebags prosper, content and smug. Despite the clear common sense of it, God has not arranged the universe so that bad things only happen to us when we are being bad and good things always happen to us when we are being good. And that is confusing and infuriating.

Why don't we live in a fair world?

I don't know.

But here is a picture of an unfair world I love . . .

We did not want to, but we disturbed the earth a lot when we built a small cabin out in the foothills of the Great Smokies several years ago. Now we try to make up for the home invasion by living lightly and being unobtrusive neighbors to the locals, mostly turkeys and deer.

One early spring afternoon my husband and I took a grocery sack and a trowel and walked around looking for some galax—the shiny, wine-red, heart-shaped leaves that peek out all winter long under the brown and the dead—to transplant near the cabin. The walking is easy because the land was logged for hardwoods sixty years ago, and the old logging roads have now become soft leaf-mold paths meandering around the property. The loggers must have left behind all the crooked trees, because the biggest hardwood trees are "catawampus" as my grandfather used to say, and we like that.

So that was sixty years ago. Then a long time after the logging—maybe twenty-five years ago—a fire ran up one side of our ridge. The state forester who came to talk with us about forest management had been a young whippersnapper firefighter and had actually been involved in fighting the blaze, so he showed us where the fire had raged. It had probably been started by lightning and driven by wind—sort of a God's-fault fire.

So today you can see where the flames licked around the trees, since some of the trunks are hollowed out a few feet above the ground, like giant wooden doughnuts with big bites taken out. And yet even the hollow trees bud and leaf in spite of themselves. And the oldest, crookedest ones keep on keeping on in defiance of the odds.

Of course trees age and die, evidently without complaint. If it's not the old hardwoods dying of fire or logging, then it's the pines when pine beetles blow in. Five or six years ago all around East Tennessee, the pine beetles showed up and sucked the life out of a lot of pines except, thank God, for the stately white pines. We bought our property in the middle of that epidemic and decided to build our cabin where a grove of pines was dying anyway. So all around our cabin the forest tips back and forth from mostly pine to mostly hardwood and back, living and dying the great crooked cycles and hollow circles of Appalachian ridge forests.

The forester told us that even fire spreads life. In the mystery of living and dying, in the very heat of a new fire, pine seeds hidden for decades in the cones of trees rotting on the forest floor will be released and new pines will shoot up and eventually shade little spindly hardwoods—until the beetles circle by or the fire blazes or the logger swings an ax and the whole thing repeats itself.

Wave upon wave upon wave of the living and the dying and the lives of the trees and the wildflowers and the grasses and the animals and the fire and the frogs and the little flying bugs, all the mystery of the forest worlds in worlds upon worlds, serving each other and killing each other and feeding each other—so beautiful and mysterious is the life and death and life again of all God's creation. And not a twig, not a leaf rustles to protest.

Perhaps we would live holier and wiser and more loving lives if we got paid for good behavior with good rewards. Or. Or perhaps we would never ever live to be holier and wiser and more loving if we had a God who kept us on a payroll rather than a God who just keeps us, in season and out, so that all the while of your little life and my little life and on into eternity we have the freedom and the possibilities of becoming more and more the unique persons we are created to be, and to love others and God in the ways each of us alone can offer.

You may be the one to spot the burning bush and start a freedom march. You may be the one to spot a forest fire and stop a

catastrophe. And together all of us are capable of so much fruitful-
ness for God in the world God has given us to love.

The questions of fairness haunt us but to base your faith on
fairness in the forests of the universe will break your heart. The
question is not, Will we die at a fair time? Or, If we sin will we die
sooner? The question is instead, Will we dare to live? So that
when we die the life is there—to be transformed, transfigured, re-
created—new me, new you, new creation. This is the gospel of
Jesus Christ.

I think Jesus invites us to get off the payroll. It doesn't work and
to bet your life that life will be fair will break your heart and kill
your spirit. And evidently God has something so much richer, so
much more eternal, so much more for us. The God of the
Appalachian forest shows us just a glimmer of the beauty and the
mystery and the awe of life and death where nothing is lost, nothing is wasted, nothing dishonored. Think how horrible a forest
would be full of perfectly fake pines and fake maples and fake
hemlocks and fake galax, when all the while the real and crooked
and catawampus and hollowed out and mossed over are ever more
thrilling.

By the way, when Carroll and I got back to the cabin and walked
over to where we wanted to plant the galax right outside the screen
porch, there were worlds of living galax already there. We just hadn't
bothered to look at the riches right under our noses. Go and don't
do likewise.

For Your Reflection

What are the cycles and circles in your life right now?
What would it look like to be off the payroll?

Bama

Solomon to God: Give your servant a hearing heart.

1 KINGS 3:9 (LITERAL TRANSLATION)

MY GRANDMOTHER BEGAN TO ENTER a world of silence shortly after the birth of her first child. She was twenty-eight years old. Her loss of hearing was gradual and unstoppable at that time, shortly after World War I. The doctors said there's nothing we know to do, and by the time she was in her mid-thirties with four little children, she could not hear their voices or much of anything else, for that matter.

She refused to use one of those trumpet things you held up to your ear. She said they were for old people and they didn't work anyway. I have seen photographs of her back then and she was beautiful and maybe a little vain.

Someone sent her some kind of large magic electric box to be set on a table in a central location, and it would amplify the sound, sort of. So she sat at the dinner table with the box and the four children chattering away and my grandfather presiding, beaming over the whole scene, and she was often baffled. She never did learn to read lips well. Her children look back and wonder if maybe she just couldn't get anybody to stay still long enough to let her practice on them. But you know how it is when you are in a family. You just sort of live along and take the givens of the family—like a mother who can't hear you—for granted.

She watched their mouths and she caught a few words, usually just the word to lead her in the wrong direction, demonstrating how close comedy lives to catastrophe. Everybody else would be hearing a story about Cousin Lillie dying of embarrassment because her petticoat fell off in the grocery store while my grandmother only heard the part about Cousin Lillie dying.

So my grandmother missed a lot, except I am sure she heard my grandfather's laugh or rather she felt his laugh. It was so big and booming, my grandfather's laugh, that surely she could feel the vibrations in the table and the floor.

And so her world was almost silent with a rather small though loving population—her family, her mother and sisters and cousins and such. A few close friends—Mrs. Foote, Mrs. Kramer. Myrtle. Of course the husband and the children. They loved her and they tried intermittently to keep her connected and tell her why they were laughing or crying or scared or whatever. But it was a lot of trouble and it was hard to catch her up on the news or help her get the joke and she got left out a lot.

Of course I wasn't around back then so I don't really know how the silence formed her. Probably not even the ones who were there, who knew her and loved her best, probably not even they could understand the pain and the mystery and the holiness. Surely nobody can understand how God works in all things, even loss, even isolation, even silence. None of us can understand how God is in all that.

All we know is that God made a promise to us, a promise in a life and then a promise on a cross. And the promise is that God is here, sometimes as small as a tiny seed, sometimes as hidden as a treasure in a grassy field, sometimes as mixed in to the pain and the chaos and the disappointments of our lives as the yeast is mixed into the dough. God is here, hidden, imperceptible, sometimes silent, often in the disguise of insignificance. But God is with us,

Emanuel, even when we don't know how to ask for help or what to ask for. Even then in our muteness, God is here in the silence for us and in us, with sighs too deep and silent for words.

By the time I knew my grandmother she was in her early sixties. Tiny, formidable, still lovely. She hummed a lot. Low and soft, she almost always hummed—I guess some melody of the universe only she could hear. Out of her silence, I think she hummed, usually a cheerful comfortable sound, unless she spotted something untoward like a crooked hem or a jar of jelly that had clouded. Or a grandchild misbehaving. Then the hum glided into a minor key until she straightened out whatever had gone awry.

She hummed and sometimes she groaned. And often she touched. She stroked. Her fingers were cool and soft on your forehead or your palm or your back. We would sit as close to her as we could and listen to her read a fairy tale or one of the Oz books or my lifelong favorite, *Ferdinand the Bull.* I can see my little brother, about six years old and pretty much of a beast, I can see him laid out blissful and quiet while she read to us and tickled the bottoms of his feet.

By then she had a real hearing aid. She called it her "telephone." It had an earpiece attached by a wire to a little machine about the size of a cigarette lighter that she kept pinned to her slip right above her heart. Sometimes there was static and it made fierce crackling noises and whistled. Then she would cut it off because it was just too annoying and confusing. And she cut it off if she was bored. At large gatherings, she mastered the art of the interested look and the encouraging nod, and all the time, I knew she'd cut her hearing aid off, and I sometimes envied her.

But if there was silence and if you looked right at her and if you talked right to her heart, well, she could hear everything you wanted to tell her. She listened with her heart and she could hear way down deep, and she could hold in her heart just what you wanted and needed her so badly to know.

In the Hebrew language, when the young king Solomon asks God for help, what he asks for as the greatest treasure of all is, in the Hebrew, not an understanding mind, as you often see his request translated. Instead what Solomon asks for is a listening heart.

And so the Hebrews knew and they taught Jesus that a listening heart is the doorway in. A heart that listens is the beginning of prayer, of faith, of depth, of real life. Not a head full of answers but a heart opened up, waiting, questioning, listening for the One who is always near, sometimes in the silence, sometimes in just the whisper of the almost still, small wind.

My grandmother's world never got very big. She traveled and read, but her day-to-day world was small. It was frustrating for her to connect with strangers or to be in a crowd. It tired her out to try, and so she didn't. And she didn't suffer fools gladly or any other way. And sometimes she could be mean as a snake, even to those she loved. So she wasn't perfect by any stretch of anybody's imagination. And her world was small. Her family and a few friends, Mrs. Foote, Mrs. Kramer, and Myrtle.

And her Sunday school class. She loved her Sunday school class. For fifty years or so she was in that class almost every Sunday morning of her life. And the last fifteen years or so she was the teacher, retiring in her eighties. They say she had a gift and touched people. Surely the gift came out of the silence. She listened to the questions of her heart and she studied the Scriptures and she thought about the Word in the silence in which she lived. And out of that she taught.

And so she was a teacher—in that Sunday school class or making mayhaw jelly or playing little casino or double solitaire after supper (not on Sunday, of course) or snuggling up together reading in the swing or humming while she mended your dress or crying when you told her something sad. She was a teacher of the Word that wells up out of silence to hearts that will listen and then spills out into life, wise and true.

A life lived. Not much drama. No great deeds of daring. Just a touch here. A hum there. Just a heart open and listening. A life lived, small, insignificant. Like a mustard seed. Or yeast in the dough. Or a treasure hidden in a grassy field.

How silently, how silently the wondrous gift is given!
So God imparts to human hearts the blessings of his heaven.
No ear may hear his coming, but in this world of sin,
Where meek souls will receive him, still the dear Christ enters in.

For Your Reflection

Who has a hearing heart in your life?
Whom do you find difficult to hear?

The Fisherman

Follow me, and I will make you fish for people.

MATTHEW 4:19

LET ME REMEMBER BACK twenty-five years. I am in my early thirties and back in church, having been on a ten-year sabbatical wandering far from my childhood Sunday habits to the land of the Academy Award Theater, a fabulous selection of old movies shown at the irresistible hour of ten o'clock every Sunday morning.

So how did I find myself in a parish? A friend invited me to church. She thought I would enjoy a Sunday school class about Southern writers called the Christ-Haunted South. I wish everybody knew how much difference a humble, no-pressure invitation can make. I don't know why I accepted but I did, and I met her at the door and went in and found home.

I have thought over the years about what attracted me to St. Anne's. Oh, there was lots. The interesting talk and the willingness to question. The warmth and sophistication of the congregation. The comfort with ambiguity, the tolerance of the different. The priest who used the wisdom of modern psychology and the passion of social justice to make the Scripture come alive for me for the first time. So you know what happened. I soak this in for a while and I'm looking around at this kind and vibrant congregation, and I am thinking, hey, this church stuff looks great. Looks pretty easy, too. I believe I will go and get myself ordained.

Soooooooooooo. In Atlanta, thank God, we had a preseminary process, though not a perfect one by any stretch of the imagination. I recently met a fine pastor a decade later who got kicked out by that very same preordination process because he was "too young." He went somewhere else. And we learned. Now we have a bunch of grumpy old priests like me and we would kill for some young ones to share the load and balance the insurance costs.

At any rate, I go through the process, which, since we had a surplus of clergy then, consisted of doing a number of things meant to make you miserable enough to quit. For instance, you had to meet with a group including all the other aspirants every Tuesday night for about a year. There were two supervisors who had the power to say yes or no to your moving forward, and I didn't like that at all. After all, if getting ordained was something I wanted to do, what did anybody else have to do with it? (I wince looking back.) Perhaps inevitably, given human nature, what was supposed to be a vocational discernment process became a win-the-prize process for me and I believe for many others down through the years.

Thus the interior conversation: How can I—let's see—look very open to the process and yet look very determined to move forward? Look sensitive but not too? Seem passionate but not crazy? Be in touch with my anger but not lethally? Love Jesus but be calm and attractive about it? It was one of those dances, if you know what I mean—kind of like a job interview—only in this one, it seemed like the door was opening or shutting for good.

All the time I was going through the vocational training process, I thought, well I will get through this mess and then go back to St. Anne's or some other spiffy place that always has plenty of money and plenty of interesting people and lots of vision and like that. So there I was.

Fortunately, someone had spotted the shiny and wonderful myth that I had so casually draped over the whole state of Christ's church and over my own vocation, and the powers that be decided to fix that. So they sent me out to the least shiny parish with the scrawniest little unshiny priest you ever saw. Bob Fisher.

He couldn't have weighed 110 pounds soaking wet and looked just like a plucked chicken and he smoked like a chimney and he said to me pretty early on that he was a recovering alcoholic as if that was supposed to explain something. Little did I know it meant he knew what a faith community was supposed to be.

And the church was in an unmemorable building way out in one of the small towns ringing and ruined by Atlanta. And the members of the congregation were working stiffs and they weren't interested in chatting about the Christ-Haunted South since they were in the financially haunted mode, trying to make the mortgage and hold down the extra job and keep the kids from skipping school.

Bob didn't actually have office hours during which people came to commune with him. Instead, he rode around in his little crummy car, smoking those cigarettes, and he took me with him. And we visited. I had thought that when a priest visited it was because some big thing had happened and you were coming in to tell folks what the Word of God was on the situation. I had thought what it means to do this job is to just glide from one fascinating crisis to the next, and to respond with wisdom and compassion and then the crisis would somehow be fixed and you would ride on off into the sunset or the next fascinating crisis, depending on what your calendar said.

But not ol' Bob Fisher. He just sort of stopped in. And he would say, Hey how're you? And the visitee—the deaf old man or the middle-aged tubby guy or the young mom with the baby whining—they didn't have big, fascinating crises. They just had lives. And ol' Bob didn't drop the Word on them. He just sort of grunted. And listened. And grunted some more. And then we would chug on, not driven by the calendar or the crisis, but staying a while or moseying on in response to the rhythm of the talk.

I didn't get what he was doing, but now I look back over my shoulder and see him smoking and see my illusions about the priesthood and the church going up in smoke as well. And in the place of my illusions I see the first glimmerings for me of the primal gifts of Christian community—compassion and endurance and reconciliation—of which ol' Bob was a master. He did me and the church more good in figuring out whether I was cut out for ordination than ten years of group gropes.

He is dead now. I forget about him for months at a time. And then he wafts through my mind, and I am better for it. God rest his soul.

For Your Reflection

Who has mentored you in the faith?
If you are part of a community of faith—why that one?
If you are not part of a community of faith—why not?

Normal

Ask, and it will be given you; seek, and you will find;
knock, and the door will be opened.

MATTHEW 7:7 (LITERAL TRANSLATION)

AS I MENTIONED IN an earlier reflection, a recent sabbatical took a strange turn when I fell out on the sidewalk in Natchez, Mississippi, and spent the next two months regathering my wits and having medical tests rather than the planned program of doing a little writing and traveling and even a little work learning about the mystery and blessing of reconciliation in the Episcopal Church after the Civil War.

I had experienced an intense allergic reaction so now I take allergy shots just like everybody else in East Tennessee. As I told our vestry, my brain—after a hiatus—is working exactly to the level and in the same ways it did before, so we are all stuck with that.

In that return vestry meeting, somebody said, well you didn't get anything out of your sabbatical. You didn't get any of your to-do list done. But looking over my shoulder I realize that I got exactly what I asked God for, just in a startling package. I suspect this happens more times than any of us recognize.

I asked God for rest. I was deeply rested, perhaps in a way I wouldn't have been if I had been full steam ahead.

I asked God for time with my growing up family. I spent a month in the places and with the people of my childhood. During that time I received a phone call from a total stranger who had heard that I wanted to know about my paternal grandfather, dead long before I was born, and she knew some stories about his mentorship of young people interested in getting into nursing or doctoring and his commitment to the practice of good medicine in those days when there wasn't much for docs to do but care and watch a lot. He had a semifamous temper that flared when people did not get the care they needed. My father also had that fierce side of compassion and I need more of it.

So I got to know an otherwise unknowable grandfather through the kindness of a stranger, and I spent time with old friends. I remember spending the afternoon with two of my closest girlhood friends—one, a very beautiful woman, now the chief antifraud officer at a large Mississippi bank. She loves it and literally can smell cheaters coming a mile off. The other woman is just a mess— mentally ill, missing teeth, institutionalized, extremely anxious. We were actually sitting out in the yard of her group home watching goats in the field next to the building.

The goats were a pleasant diversion while we three found each other. But better than the goats next door was the chance to witness the deeper than any goats and sheep compassion offered by the antifraud woman to the messed up one. They share a friendship that has now lasted since high school and through their being college roommates (and at that time it was the antifraud expert who was in the trouble of her life). Gail has been institutionalized over and over again. She is hard to find, hard to keep up with, hard to love when found. But underneath the manipulation, the paranoia, the intense self-absorption, she is not a fraud, and the antifraud expert loves her persistently, faithfully, the way Jesus asks us to love, seventy times seven.

And so on that one afternoon, I was part of my mentally ill friend coming to the surface through her illness and weariness to connect with us, just for a moment, clear and nonanxious, best she's done this year, the fraud investigator says. I did not know the routine or the sacraments. I didn't know the eucharist would be the offering of chocolate and cigarettes. I didn't know what to say or how to help. We were just three friends reaching way back, and I wasn't supposed to even pretend to orchestrate the spirit. And that was a strange and gentle relief.

For that is the third thing I asked God for. I asked God to help me—this is hard to describe—I asked God to help me be just a normal person instead of a clergyperson. For, when you have worn a clergy collar for going toward twenty years and you have lived— sometimes well, sometimes poorly—into the role that I have lived into, then you have spent a lot of time in the middle of other people's lives, often present during other people's high points or low points. The birth, the baptism, the wedding, the marital or vocational crisis, the spiritual angst, the illness, the funeral—those are major points of contact for me with others. I remember a priest friend of mine wore rubber-soled shoes because, really, an ordained person needs to walk very quietly since we so often stand on holy ground where God and another are meeting.

So I asked God for normal where nobody had any expectations of me to be anything but myself. And I got it, just ordinary old bumper car living. I am not saying I liked all of it but I got it. Besides catching up with cousins and people I rarely see, I met a long dead grandfather. And the afternoon with the goats and the fraud investigator and the lost sheep—well that stays with me, a wellspring of faith.

I did find out that I like it a lot better being prayerful and deep about other people's mortality rather than my own. So I am back to wearing the collar—it is a lot easier on the nerves. And yet surely I say my prayers a little fuller now and wear the collar a little looser.

The next time you are with an ordained person, please remember how human we are, at least I hope and pray we are, and how hard it is sometimes to hang on to that. We just may need to be reminded from time to time that we all walk (and sometimes crawl and sometimes waltz) through the valley of the shadow. That is normal.

For Your Reflection

How do you relate to ordained people?
Why do we ordain people? Are they holier than normal?
Was Jesus ordained?

Feeding the Wolves Within

I do not understand my own actions. For I do not do what I want, but I do the very thing I hate. . . . I find it to be a law that when I want to do what is good, evil lies close at hand.

ROMANS 7:15, 21

A FRIEND SENT ME this legend. An elder in the Cherokee Nation was teaching his grandchildren about life. He said to them, "A fight is going on inside me, a terrible fight between two wolves. One wolf is mean-spirited and filled with fear, anger, envy, greed, arrogance, self-doubt, resentment, lies, and false pride. The other wolf is gentle in spirit and filled with trust, hope, humility, generosity, friendship, truth, compassion, and faith. This same fight is going on inside you and inside every other person, too."

The children thought a moment—picturing the wolves fighting. And one child asked his grandfather, "Which wolf will win?"

The old man replied, "The one you feed."

All cultures and faiths recognize the tension between good and evil in every human being. And that same tension is in every human community, including communities of faith. This tug of war is expressed well by the Apostle Paul who says, "When I want to do what is good, evil lies close at hand." Is that not disgustingly true?

It is a dilemma. At the age of fifty-seven, I am just barely getting a handle on my capacity to do harm, albeit not consciously, not on purpose, in my sometimes clumsy attempts to "he'p somebody."

And goodness we can get the wolves snarling in communities of faith. An experienced pastor told me a long time ago that the worst church fight he ever witnessed was over paint color. No kidding. But don't you know that the people involved in the paint debacle all thought that they were doing good for God? And yet they fed the mean-spirited wolves and people got chewed up. What church decision is worth that? What condemnation of another—be it their God-given taste in paint chips or matters more deeply of the essence of a human being—is worth the soul-danger of feeding the hate-filled wolf?

Some world religions teach that one can overcome the mean-spiritedness within by self-discipline or obedience to the laws of the faith. Others say that evil is just a mirage and that one need only remember that evil is not real. And yet another teaches letting go of all attachments so that one is less and less tempted by self-centered needs, thus rising above the evil within.

Even within Christianity, there are wildly different evil wolf-trapping strategies. Some Christians believe that one single experience of salvation is what every Christian must have. While others believe that strict adherence to the words of the Bible will kill off the evil wolf inside. And then there are those for whom the sacraments of the church—especially baptism and communion—are wolf-killers. And so it gets tempting for all of us to look at the other one and sniff and sneer, which of course feeds all our snapping self-righteous wolves who then yap for more.

Which wolf are you feeding? Is it the part of you who walks humbly with the God of justice and mercy?

I love the Cherokee legend, and I believe it has a piece of the truth. The more we feed the mean-spiritedness within us, the hungrier that old snaggletoothed wolf gets. But I just can't seem to feed my "better wolf" on my own. As Paul noticed, even the best wolves have ornery puppies, and so it goes with even our best efforts, our most generous impulses, our most stringent disciplines. When we try hardest to be good, evil really does lie close at hand.

Instead of trying to split ourselves open and just grab hold of the best parts, it seems to me that we Christians have another way—the way of humility, the way of wry and humble self-acceptance by the grace of God. And somehow in humble self-acceptance—all of us gets fed. In the Body of Christ, somehow those parts of me and you that are petty and fearful and mean get nourished by Love, too. So that for a moment or an hour or maybe for a day, in the middle of our ordinary, ornery, double-hearted lives, the peaceable kingdom comes and the wolf and the lamb and the leopard and the lion and the calf and the little child get fed and lie down together in us and among us and we know it in our hearts and in our bones.

Of course, the moment fades, the hour changes, the day turns. But the peaceable kingdom happened, does happen, and the peaceable kingdom will happen again, wolves and all.

For Your Reflection

Which part of you do you need to offer to God for healing and transformation?

How do we teach and learn self-acceptance while also asking what Jesus demands—the best of our selves?

The Easter Stuff

[O]n the first day of the week, at early dawn, they came to the tomb taking the spices that they had prepared.

LUKE 24:1

A LONGTIME FRIEND, an old soul with the unlikely name of Fifi, describes an odd experience that has happened a time or two to me as well. She has noticed that after someone you love very much dies, there is sometimes a trick of the eye and the memory. So that—when you come to the doorway of a long-familiar room or you look toward a chair in the garden or when you walk down a formerly shared path in your life and around a bend—out of the corner of your eye, you see, just for a glimpse, you just may see the one you love. Just for a moment, just in a glimmer, there almost out of the range of your vision, you almost see the one you love in an old familiar place.

And your heart lurches a little and there is a part of you that hurts from the loss again and a part of you that is thrilled, that rejoices in the illusion, in the kindly gift of the eye and the memory. And so, in little quirky parts of your heart and mind, the beloved returns to the old expected place in your life in the old familiar way. But all the time you know, well, it's just a kindly trick . . . of the memory and the eye.

This happened for me when I was visiting in my hometown and looking at a silver-haired stranger and saw my father smiling back. And then the man moved, or I did, and he went back to being a stranger. And so it goes. We love. We lose. We wonder if the loss is forever. . . .

Last spring I was not putting in a garden for the first time in years so I did the next-best thing. I went and stood in the garden department of Lowe's to smell the dirt and see the flowers nodding and watch the people fill their little wagons. There were middle-aged couples and young parents in their first nests and an old man in overalls with a rose bush. It was a beautiful East Tennessee day and all was right with the world and everybody was quietly doing their thing. And then all of a sudden out of nowhere, I hear a woman's voice bellowing: WHHHAAAARRRRRR'S THE EASTER STUFF? WHHHAAAARRRRR IZZ IT? The clerk pulls himself together and thinks for a minute and says, Well, I think the Easter stuff is in the main store, up by the cash registers. And the loud woman huffs off.

And I think, honey, I don't think the Easter stuff is at the Lowe's cash register, or the Walmart either. But where is it? Where is the Easter stuff once you get beyond the candied egg stage? Where is it once your heart has been broken, once you have loved and lost and are bereft? Where is the Easter stuff then? Or is the Easter stuff a kindly trick—a little white lie—on the level of bunnies and dyed eggs?

The women whose hearts were first broken by the crucifixion and the death—perhaps they can be our teachers. They knew that Love wouldn't be the way that they had known Love before. They couldn't just go back to the places where they saw Love before and find business as usual. They had to go on to the tomb and face the truth, which is to say they had to face the death.

The truth that they thought they would face was finality and loss and decay and death of all that matters about Love. For these truths they were prepared with spices and stoic faces and dignity in the presence of the loss. They were prepared and they brought what they could to care for dead Love, to make the death of Love as seemly and dignified as possible. And because they risked coming to face the death of Love, my God, what did they find?

What? Well, not dead love. That's for sure. The tomb was empty. And those first witnesses were totally bamboozled.

I would have thought it was the final insult. That my friends and I had come to anoint the dead body and the last insult to our love is to take away the dead body of love and throw it in a hidden ditch to lie unmourned and unburied. That the enemies of love—and there's no sense trying to pin this on one enemy of love or another there are so many enemies of love lurking in the human heart—I would have thought that the enemies of love had won again and finally, and had taken the dead body away to dishonor and oblivion.

What would you have thought? Since back then, this wasn't a story written in a leather book.

For anybody who has lived long enough to love and lose and grieve to the bone, this is no story. It is the truth of the human condition. It is the pain of being a human being to always be losing love, to always be saying goodbye to love—for we are so very mortal and to dust we shall return and all we love shall return—dust to dust, ashes to ashes. And what we try to do is make our good-byes as seemly and dignified as possible. So what I believe those women went to do that day was the best they or we could hope to do under the circumstances of being mortal. They went to the tomb and their best hope was to say good-bye fully and deeply to Love.

But the tomb was empty. And the stone was rolled away. And the dead Body of Love was gone. And that is the truth at the heart of our faith.

And that is the wonder and the miracle and the beauty and the joy. By Christ, in Christ, through Christ, our last best hope is not a seemly and dignified good-bye. Our last best hope is that the tomb was empty. Love meets death and wins.

Of course they couldn't figure it out. They didn't know what happened. They had to just stay bamboozled and wait to see what would come next. Which turns out to be, of all things, angels. God sent them the angels to help them remember the Easter stuff—though Jesus had told them all the Easter stuff before—what would happen and that Love would last. Not just last. Not just endure. The Easter stuff is the stuff of triumph. And the angels had to tell them to remember that and to go out and tell others.

Which is where we come in. We have heard the Easter stuff because the angels helped those women remember the Easter stuff. And they told their friends the Easter stuff and their friends told the next friends the Easter stuff and on and on—the Easter stuff getting told and retold, remembered and re-remembered and growing and living in love, generation after generation all the way to us. The Easter stuff is always passed on from friend to friend for when the Easter stuff passes, even an enemy becomes a friend.

So that now we get to be the ones who help each other—all our friends and even our enemies—remember and trust that love never ends. And that at the end of our days, it won't be a trick. And it won't be just a glimpse here, an illusion there, a kindly trick of eye and memory. The Easter stuff will fill our souls and we will live in love with love and through love with all we mourn—made new and raised up and brought into fullness, into perfection, into eternity.

For Your Reflection

What would you have thought and felt if you had come to the empty tomb?

Who passed on the Easter stuff to you?

Marmi

As an elder myself and a witness of the sufferings of Christ as well as one who shares in the glory to be revealed, I thank God for you elders who tend the flock of God that is in your charge.

1 PETER 5 (ADAPTATION)

MARMI MAIRS WAS an eight o'clocker. That was my first Marmi identifying marker. And I have a sort of standard operating assumption with eight o'clockers: Let sleeping dogs lie. Don't mess with the liturgy or shift the time for a summer schedule or anything, because that part of the flock seems to thrive on the same hill of the same pasture beside the same water, week in and week out and year in and year out, and that's fine.

Marmi wasn't quite five feet tall, pushing seventy when I met her six years ago—casual good-looking clothes, curly cropped hair, eyes ready to laugh or question or scowl or whatever the occasion required. She loved the University of Tennessee women's basketball team, the Lady Vols, and had her season tickets. The scowl was most often reserved for babies that dared to come to the eight o'clock and when a baby made the mistake of sitting near her, Marmi would pick herself and her pocketbook up and head to a faraway pew. For some unfathomable reason—no kidding—two of the baddest babies we have had, had parents who deliberately would go sit next to Marmi just to watch her react.

Marmi lived on a TVA lake on family land. For years she was the vice mayor of Louisville, Tennessee—or as she said the mayor of

101

vice. She was also a chemist by profession who was married late in life to a much older man, a friend of her father and mother. They had eight or nine good, good years and then she nursed him as he died. His daughter was married with children of her own by the time Marmi showed up as the stepgrandmother least likely to succeed. However, after the common-link husband/father died, Marmi and the daughter seemed to continue a pleasant though geographically distant relationship.

Marmi liked my predecessor a lot, and had breakfast with him and a group of old friends, mostly eight o'clockers, every Sunday for years and years. For some reason, she decided to give me a chance and we became friends as well. When she was diagnosed with multiple myeloma, we connected like you do.

How to say this? If you have lived a while, you have been there. You have witnessed the sufferings of Christ as well as shared in the glory to be revealed. Can you in your heart and mind and spirit pull up right now one of the ones who taught you, who has been Christ for you, who has revealed for you the suffering and the glory of the Lord and the mystery of life and death and life again?

Marmi was such a one for me. She set her considerable affairs in order—she called up the diocesan camp director and told him to come get her pontoon boat and one of the happy moments in that long, grueling, eventually agonizing time was when he took her on a last ride and the boat had new cushions that said Grace Point, the camp's name.

And she called up her best friend in Philadelphia—and they met in New York and had a ball, and Marmi came home worn to a nub and went in the hospital and never came out.

Marmi did not suffer fools gladly, and she thought the church was rather foolish and timid in the way we encouraged people to give money. Marmi gave away five percent of her estate to seven different ministries and charities, including our parish, so 35 percent of her money has gone to work where she had served and been served. And she told me to tell the story of her planning and giving so that others would do likewise and so I tell you and ask you to pass her witness on.

And then in the little drab hospital room, she went at the disease like a prizefighter and fought and fought and fought. She figured out how to get the nurses to love her by always keeping Snickers bars in her room. And after a while she didn't even need the candy—they just loved her guts and her orneriness and her authenticity. And even better Marmi let Leslie, the pleasant semi-stranger stepdaughter, fight with her. And Leslie left her Atlanta life and was up here for weeks on end. And a carpenter, a parish friend, stayed in the hospital room half the day so Leslie could go home and sleep.

Me, I hung in with her on one level but I chickened out on another, like you do sometimes one way or the other. And so I went to Marmi's internist, also mine, and I said I have never ever ever seen pain like this. Can't you knock her out, put her out of all this pain? And the young doc looked me straight in the eye and she said, She's doing work she wants to do and she is doing it her way and we've got to stand it with her. And we did—the worst I've witnessed except for some AIDS deaths—and Marmi triumphed in the sufferings of Christ and the glory of everlasting love was revealed. And she went out knowing how she was loved and loving back, too. I don't need to go see an old movie about the sufferings of Christ. I have been witness in the Body.

Think of your teachers and remember and thank God for them and for the terrible gift of the Christian vocation of witness. What amazing realities people are called to witness, and people of faith are called to name. What we have seen—horrific suffering, courage, laughter in the face of the awe-ful, agape friendship beyond any measure, gallantry, terrible, terrible, terrible sadness, doubt, despair, wonder, acceptance, reconciliation, peace at the end, and the grace of God that passes all our understanding. Elisabeth Kübler-Ross doesn't know the half of it. We get to witness the presence of the Lord in unspeakable and holy ways.

And sometimes, we let the glory in. Thanks, Marmi, I know Jesus better because of you.

For Your Reflection

Who are the teachers of stewardship—in all the meanings of that word—in your life?

Who has revealed to you the sufferings of Christ? The glory?

Swapping Places

He maketh me to lie down in green pastures:
he leadeth me beside the still waters.

PSALM 23:2 (KJV)

ONE SUMMER I SWITCHED PLACES with a parish priest from England. We e-mailed back and forth for six months or so, working out the details, and then coordinated our airplane tickets so that I stayed an extra day in Maryville to meet him and then my husband stayed a day or two longer to get him through the jet lag and orient him to our car, house, and highways and byways. His wife also waited in St. Albans, an ancient and interesting town a little north of London, to set me up with their car and their house.

From the moment John galloped through the security gate, it was pretty obvious that he did not need much orientation. I thought this guy can find his way around East Tennessee. Or East Jerusalem. Or East Back of Beyond. John was basically one of those people who came into the world already at home in the universe.

He was a huge man, six and a half feet tall, with a grin to match, and an eager interest in all he surveyed. Within ten minutes he knew the names of our grown children and the highlights of their stories. I think he probably knew the names of the grandchildren we don't even have yet. By the time we got home, he had several day trips lined up. Within a matter of hours, he was driving on the right side of the road like a pro and he had found a shortcut to the vegetable market, which he kindly showed us. Our old cat, whose usual greeting to strangers is to open one eye, inspect, and then go back to sleep in disgust, twirled around John's feet and purred like a banshee.

John just plunged into the parish the next day at church as we worked our way though the Sunday Eucharists. His voice rang strong and true in worship, and afterwards, he connected with people as if he had a built-in tuning fork for relationships—joking with this one, gentle with that one. I don't believe the man ever met a stranger. He just was at ease in the universe—not in an obnoxious show-off way—but at ease as if he expected that everywhere he was, there would be some kind of green pasture and plenty of cool, clear water.

Believe it or not, he didn't even get on my nerves. If you know what I mean.

I wish I could say I replicated his smooth landing upon my arrival in England. I did not. His wife cheerily greeted me at the airport and I believe I grunted in reply. How do people do that? How do people fly all night or all day into another time, another world, and arrive with their wits about them? We drove the hour and a half to St. Albans with her courageously holding up her end of the conversation and me responding as if I were waiting for my lawyer to arrive. As we whipped along on the absolute wrong side of the road in their gorgeous brand-new red car, I do remember thinking, I surely hope these people do not plan to hand the keys of this beauty over to me. Surely they have a clunker at home that won't mind a dent or two.

Nope. We arrive at their lovely home, walk in past their two kitties who do look up in disgust, put my bags down, and at Tish's fairly firm invitation, get back in their brand-new car for a driving lesson. Did you get that? The car was spanking brand-new and horribly expensive looking. I did not have a good feeling about this. My husband, who loves me, won't ride with me even in America because he says it's "painful."

Tish took us around the neighborhood, a picture postcard everywhere we turned. I could not see the green pastures and the still waters for worrying about the impossibly narrow street where at any moment I would soon be behind the wheel.

Did I say the car was brand-new? And—oh, agony—stick shift?

The suspense was over pretty quickly. I was so nervous, I clipped a mailbox within a quarter of a mile of getting behind the wheel. I now have seen the power and the glory of the British stiff upper lip. After the shock (well, it was no shock to me—I have been running into mailboxes and such for forty years) we saw that no damage had been done, thank God, and we decided maybe I would use the bus system at least until my husband got there.

The trip turned out to be lovely. I met wonderful people, though I missed some moments I still regret because of shyness and laziness. I was invited to preach and celebrate in a space where people have been worshipping Jesus since the eleventh century. I heard evensong almost every day. I haunted the British Library. It was truly once in a lifetime. But I carried my uneasiness in navigating strange territory with me and John carried his indefatigable at-homeness. For though John and I swapped places, we did not swap interior worlds.

If I had it to do over again, could I be more like John? Nope. But I might be more aware and comfortable with my own boundaries, including the one about not driving someone else's brand-new, horribly expensive car, which would free me to be a more relaxed visitor. For in truth the green pastures and the still waters are always available for anybody who is willing to be pretty much exactly the sheep God made her to be.

For Your Reflection

What kind of visitor are you?

How do you tell someone who is trying to be kind that you do not want to accept the gift?

Where is Jesus in our hospitality?

Living on Your Expectations

Now hope that is seen is not hope. For who hopes for what is seen?
But if we hope for what we do not see, we wait for it with patience.

ROMANS 8:24–25

MY MOTHER'S PATERNAL grandfather is a mythical figure in our family. I have a photograph of him probably in his late thirties, very posed, standing in an ornate archway with what looks to be velvet drapery flowing behind him. He is turned to the three-quarter view with one hand on the back of a chair and the other hand in the pocket of his coat and his shoes are shined to mirrors. His face is handsome, serious, inquisitive, as if he has just asked the camera a question and is politely waiting for the reply. He died when Mother was two so she never really knew him, just his legend. And his legend was told and retold in our family in these words: great-grandfather lived on his expectations.

That is what he did. That was his full-time job. Oh, Mother said he did something mysterious with cotton but evidently not very profitably. But his expectations—he knew how to live on those, and stream through the seasons at peace and happy in the compact world of Natchez, Mississippi, raising his four boys in the country and being the adored companion of his wife and visiting with his family and friends and being a neighbor and a staunch church-man. Not anxious or hurried, not cross or demanding, least of all of himself. And never very solvent or very successful, but pleased with life. And everybody just understood that he lived on his expectations.

You might ask, And what were his expectations? Surely like you and me, he had a lot of expectations, starting with the sun rising every morning and the children behaving, and his neighbors respecting his boundaries and his Presbyterian Church not being too obstreperous and turkey hunting season rolling around. Like you and me, I am sure he had a lot of expectations but there was one special one, perhaps not that helpful, which would be the expectation of inheriting his great-aunt's money.

Like a lot of people down through the ages, he went to church and was a moral person but when push came to shove, rumor had it that his song of trust was not just "Come thou, long-expected Jesus," but also "Come thou, long-expected letter from the Philadelphia lawyer of my rich old aunt." Which could only come as a result of a regrettable but necessary funeral. The old lady, however, was hale and hearty—who would wish her less? And in the meantime, life went on. And my great-grandmother homeschooled her boys, actually started a little school with a few other country children and my great-grandfather continued doing the mysterious thing he did with cotton. And it all worked out.

I don't know how they did it, but he didn't worry about the present; instead he just lived along into the abundance that he was always expecting. And somehow when you live contentedly on your expectations—of joy, of hope, of kindness, of goodwill, of enough—well, abundance of life comes.

I asked Mama if his wife and children kidded about him living on his expectations and she said, My heavens, no. But his friends and relations remarked on it from time to time sort of fondly, I believe, hinting at his foolishness, his laziness.

I think Jesus liked him. For didn't Jesus love the lilies of the field and the birds of the air whose trust of the Creator is so wired into their very beings that religious piety would be an affectation?

I want to hold up my great-grandfather and say, Good for him. It might be worth a moment to admire the grace of happy people, especially when we have got all the worries of life sloshing over us every day, reality knocking on our door, worries abounding, deals to make, bills to pay, crises to attend to. When I wonder about what kind of person would live at peace on their expectations, I like the picture that emerges.

By the way, the old lady lived almost forever and the money was not that much. So what?

Come thou long expected Jesus.
Born to set thy people free.
From our fears and sins release us.
Let us find our rest in thee.

For Your Reflection

What are the expectations you live on?

What would you like people to say about you in the generations to come?

Who is the Judge?

God did not give us a spirit of cowardice, but rather a spirit of power and of love and of self-discipline.

2 TIMOTHY 1:7

THERE IS A LITTLE VOICE that speaks inside our heads. Just picture a little judge sitting in your head in a little tiny black robe with an even tinier gavel. And depending on your genes and your growing-up influences, you start out with either a pretty pessimistic judge or a hopeful one. My father, for instance, would look at a perfectly blue sky and remark, Ooohh Tobi—he often addressed his concerns to our surly schnauzer—so he would say, Oohhhh, Tobi-boy, I think there's a bad front heading our way. My mother, on the other hand, even now in her mid-eighties, could be in the middle of a hurricane and ignore it if she needed to or just wanted to. So our little judges have responses that have been handed to us, and of course we develop our own.

But that little judge inside of you doesn't just read the weather. That little ego judge inside you judges people. And somehow over the years you and your little judge have trained each other for better and worse to look at the people around you and decide who is trustworthy or not, dangerous or not, competent or not, lovable or not, liable to be helpful to you or to cause you trouble. It goes without saying that, with and without malice, different judges assess people and situations and spoken words in remarkably different ways.

113

And of course the little judge inside me is always judging and misjudging me. And the little ego judge inside you is always judging and misjudging you. And frankly, that is the heart of the matter. For if we cannot see the log in our own eye, as somebody who loves us once said, how are we going to see the splinter in the other guy's eye? So I want to ask you, How well do you think your little judge does in judging you?

I think most of us are beyond lousy at judging ourselves, which of course makes us even lousier at judging other people or the world at large. I know I am a poor self-judge and I am highly suspicious of you. For one thing, of course, we miss our shadows, our sins. For to see one's sin is as hard as to see the back of one's head. It is right there, but we cannot see it and even looking in a mirror distorts and reverses it so that what looks like where the sin is, it is often not. So we are bad at seeing our shadows, our sins, and that blindness causes so much needless, endless pain in ourselves, our relationships, our world.

But the even bigger problem is that our little black-robed judges are even more inept at seeing our goodness. We are mostly just terrible at recognizing our gifts and celebrating the strengths God has given us. And so we are not good at trusting the One who made us to have made us well and strong and to have made each of us with intention and for holy purposes in the world. When we listen to our little judges we are, God forgive us, cowards and we are afraid we are not strong enough or good enough or important enough to make a difference in ourselves, much less the universe.

But. Our little judges who sit in our heads in the tiny black robes need not have the last word. In the New Testament, the writer of the letter to young Timothy told him what I want to claim. At our birth, God gave you and me a spirit with power, with love, with self-discipline. We are created by the love of God and through the grace of Christ to wake up every morning and say, I contain within myself the Holy Spirit of the living God. And when I claim that holy connection beyond my little judge, I claim the power of God in my very being to direct myself to love and to serve.

A deacon in the diocese told me a story about some members of the French Resistance during World War II. They were captured by the Nazis and instead of being shot like so many others they were sent to work in a munitions factory to make bombs. And of course they were sick at heart knowing that the bombs they were building would kill and maim the very people they wanted to save. So they thought and thought and the religious ones prayed and as the days went by they began to stay awake at night and rip up their sheets and newspapers and the little bits of toilet paper they had and scraps of books, including the Bibles and their precious writing paper. And the next day they would pretend to stuff the bombs with the explosives but instead they would fill them with little scraps of paper and fabrics and always with a note that read "we are doing the best we can with what we have and where we are."

We are doing the best we can with what we have and where we are.

And they were because they used the hearts and the heads and the hands that God had given them. And even in an enemy bomb factory they worked the best they could with what they had and where they were for the triumph of justice toward the day of peace. And that by the grace of God is all it takes.

The disciples said to Jesus, Increase our faith. As if Jesus might just throw some fairy dust on them or a little voodoo or even give them a foolproof manual for faith. Heck, I don't blame them, do you? I would love—especially in scary tough times—I would love to say to Jesus, Lay it on us. Increase our faith. But what Jesus said to them and to us is this: You have already got all the faith you need. If you would but trust that God made you with power for love to serve, you could do anything. You could pick up a tree and throw it across the street, which seems like a kind of silly idea, but

Jesus is just telling us to get it, get with it, claim it, use it. The power of the Spirit of God to love, to serve, is imprinted in your very being. And that's the only power that lasts and the only power with eternal consequences. Use it. Or lose it.

So what say we tell that little judge who sits in our heads with a little black robe and tiny gavel—let's tell him or her to refer all our cases to the Higher Court. Where the One who judges us most fairly, most truly just happens to be the One who made us in the first place and loves us most completely, most deeply. This is not new information. Jesus lived and died to tell us this.

Or as the mentor in the faith said to Timothy, *God did not give us a spirit of cowardice, but rather a spirit of power and of love and of self-discipline.*

Claim it.

For Your Reflection

Where in your life do you need to claim that you are doing the best you can with what you have?

Who is your judge?

The River

WHEN I WAS A LITTLE GIRL in Mississippi, I thought that the Mississippi River belonged just to our state due to the name.

Actually I thought the river belonged to the bluff town, Natchez, Mississippi, which is where I saw it most often. Sometimes we would come into town from my grandfather's place in the country and go park at the Ramada Inn where you can see the bridge and the barges as long as two football fields—engines chugging hard to fight upstream in the deep channel or effortlessly floating down. Or we would stop by the lovely old town cemetery, which sits even higher on the bluff, a place of peace and the long view toward the big northward bend in the river. Some of you have been to Natchez and you know that at that point the Mississippi is a mile wide and very strong, very brown. Years later when I read T. S. Eliot's line in *Four Quartets*—*I think that the river is a strong brown god*—I thought of course the river is a strong brown god because the Mighty Mississippi River at Natchez was the meaning of river for me.

My favorite view of the river was on the enormous bridge to Louisiana, high up, suspended in the heavens. I can still hear the whine and rhythm of the tires rolling on some sort of metal grid, maybe to keep you alert—youah, youah, youah, youah—as if you need stimulus when you are hundreds of feet in the air over a writhing water serpent. And we children would gaze out over the enormous swirls and eddies as big as houses, our eyes wide in awe of the sheer power of the water, and we would try to hold our breath all the way across the bridge but we never did—too wide, too long, impossible to cross in one breath.

And then we would descend into sleepy, flat, dusty Vidalia, Louisiana—so susceptible to the river's whims and floods, cowering behind huge earthen levees built to—hah!—manage the water. I always felt sorry for Louisiana, since the Mississippi River clearly didn't belong to them. Ferriday, the next town over, had instead— probably still does have—a huge banner that said "Welcome to the Home of Jerry Lee Lewis." But we had Elvis and Faulkner and Bessie Smith and Eudora Welty and B. B. King and Robert Johnson and Muddy Waters. And of course the river.

Little did I know that—oh, yes—the river had its way in the flatlands of Louisiana but the river also flooded my state's delta dirt, which is actually why it's so rich. And even in Natchez two streets full of those beautiful antebellum homes and part of the seemingly impervious cemetery would slide down the bluff some years later and return to the river. Nor did I know that "my" river belonged first to red-golden-skinned peoples who had been living on its banks for five thousand years, so my family, too, had come as unwanted carpetbaggers. And little did I understand that the river belongs to Minnesota as well and the Dakotas, and that the white snows of the north become the brown eddies of the south. And that the river belongs to the Wild West and Virginia, to thirty-three states, 2,300 miles of belonging. In some places it is so tiny that a child could step across.

And little did I know that forty-five years later I would live on a street in East Tennessee with the Little River wandering past the foot of our hill and that I would serve in a church overlooking

Pistol Creek. And that our sparkling clear and cold creek-rivers—by way of the Tennessee River swinging up through Kentucky and into the Ohio—flow down, down, down, down through American heartland to Memphis, Vicksburg, Natchez, New Orleans. So that every day Pistol Creek of Maryville, Tennessee, becomes part of the strong brown water that grumbles past the stone angels guarding the graves of my family high on a windy bluff in Natchez, Mississippi. For here, as everywhere, the living waters that rain down from heaven return to the land and the creek and the lake and the river and the source of all of life.

And so it is with us. We are part of a reality that is so much bigger than we ever comprehend. And the river of our lives starts back further in space and time and spirit than we will ever know and goes where we cannot imagine—each of us adding our little drops of spirit, of energy, of life to the future. And the river never belongs to us, ever. That's a silly notion. How can a drop or even a wave own the way and the truth and the life of the river? For the river belongs to God.

When we remember those who have gone before us, we thank God for their gifts and ask God to bless their lives eternally. I wonder what would they tell us about the river of life?

Of course we can't hear them now; we believe we will hear them again, even more fully, when we, too, return to the source. But with Christ Jesus as our interpreter, I wonder if they might tell us at least these three things.

First I believe those who have gone ahead of us in the river of life would say, Fear not. Fear not. There is nothing in all of creation—no flood, no drought, no dam, no mud—nothing that can separate us from the love of God flowing through the universe. For the flood feeds the seed, and the dam forces energy and opportunity. So fear not.

Second, I believe they would say to us, Find the deep channel. Go with God's flow. For if we do not deepen along the journey— with others and in ourselves—we become shallow, a mile wide and an inch deep. And then when the storm hits, we lose our way. We are none of us just enough or merciful enough or wise enough to manage the river of life. So go with God's flow. And find the deep channel.

And finally I believe they would say to us, enjoy the ride. Do not grieve for yesterday. Do not obsess about tomorrow. Be open, as our Savior Christ was, to the joy and life of this day, this hour, this moment. For in the end, nothing is lost, not a drop, not a seed, not a mote of dust, and certainly not a child of God. Because we are not alone; we are connected through Christ like drops of water in a brook, in a lake, in a river. Which means we belong to all of creation ever renewed, ever re-created by the grace of God—season after season—life to death to life to death to life—all moments leading to the next and grace washing over all, flowing by grace back toward the source of life and the sea of eternity.

For Your Reflection

What is your river like?
Where do you find the deep channel?